TOLKIEN

New
Critical
Perspectives

TOLKIEN

NEW CRITICAL PERSPECTIVES

Edited by
Neil D. Isaacs
& Rose A. Zimbardo

THE UNIVERSITY PRESS OF KENTUCKY

Robert M. Adams, "*The Silmarillion* and the Hobbit
Habit." Reprinted with permission from *The New York
Review of Books*. Copyright © 1977 Nyrev, Inc.

Paul H. Kocher, "Middle Earth: An Imaginary World,"
from *Master of Middle Earth* by Paul H. Kocher.
Copyright © 1972 by Paul H. Kocher. Reprinted by
permission of Houghton Mifflin Co. and Thames and
Hudson Ltd.

Library of Congress Cataloging in Publication Data

Main entry under title:

Tolkien, new critical perspectives.

    1. Tolkien, John Ronald Reuel, 1892-1973—Criticism
and interpretation—Addresses, essays, lectures.
I. Isaacs, Neil David, 1931-   II. Zimbardo, Rose A.
PR6039.032Z85   828'.91209   80-51015
ISBN 0-8131-1408-X

Scholarly publisher for the Commonwealth
serving Berea College, Centre College of Kentucky,
Eastern Kentucky University, The Filson Club,
Georgetown College, Kentucky Historical Society,
Kentucky State University, Morehead State University,
Murray State University, Northern Kentucky University,
Transylvania University, University of Kentucky,
University of Louisville, and Western Kentucky University.

Editorial and Sales Offices: Lexington, Kentucky 40506

For Ian, Johnny, Daniel, Adam, and Anne —
  no longer halflings, but Elven lords and
  lady in their radiant maturity

....

Preface

....

Quotations from *The Lord of the Rings* are taken from the revised edition (Boston, 1967), and we are grateful to Houghton Mifflin Company for their cooperation; citations appear parenthetically in the text by volume and page numbers. References to *The Hobbit* are to the Houghton Mifflin edition (Boston, 1938); to "On Fairy-Stories" are to *Tree and Leaf* (Boston, 1965); to "Beowulf: The Monsters and the Critics" are to *An Anthology of Beowulf Criticism,* ed. Lewis E. Nicholson (Notre Dame, Ind., 1963), pp. 51-103, and the latter essay is cited as *"Beowulf* essay." *Tolkien and the Critics* (Notre Dame, 1968) is cited as *T & C;* we are grateful to the University of Notre Dame Press for their cooperation.

For permission to reprint we are grateful to Daniel Hughes and Southern Illinois Press for "Pieties and Giant Forms in *The Lord of the Rings"* from *Shadows of Imagination,* ed. Mark R. Hillegas (1969); to Patrick Grant and the editors of *Cross Currents* for "Tolkien: Archetype and Word" (1973), pp. 365-80; to Paul Kocher, Houghton Mifflin Co., and Thames and Hudson Ltd. for the chapter from *Master of Middle Earth* by Paul H. Kocher; to Joseph McLellan and the *Washington Post* for "Frodo and the Cosmos," September 4, 1977; and to Robert M. Adams and the *New York Review of Books* for *"The Silmarillion* and the Hobbit Habit," November 24, 1977. For their original essays, revisions, and cooperation we are also grateful to all other contributors: Lionel Basney, Verlyn Flieger, David Jeffrey, Lois Kuznets, Henry Parks, and J. S. Ryan; and to Katharine Shaw and Kenneth Cherry of the University Press of Kentucky.

Neil D. Isaacs

ON THE NEED FOR WRITING TOLKIEN CRITICISM

The "effort to save Tolkien from the faddists and the
button makers," as Rose Zimbardo called our collection
first published in 1968, must go on. Indeed, now more
than ever, with the publication of a variety of material
assembled by Christopher Tolkien under the title *Silmarillion,* the distinctions between the stuff of a cult
and the objects of critical literary investigation
should be brought sharply into focus.

   Tolkien: New Critical Perspectives now appears
shortly after the passing of *The Silmarillion* from the
best-seller lists following two brief seasons in the
sun, but our emphasis remains on *The Lord of the Rings.*
We have, after all, a decade's worth of scholarly and
critical work to account for, and there is still a general understanding that the trilogy is, if not the heart
of Tolkien's work, at least head and shoulders above the
rest of his creative corpus. But it is not his only
work worthy of attention.

   During the decade a rather substantial body of
Tolkien criticism has been developed. (We considered
offering a comprehensive bibliography here, but since
Wayne G. Hammond's addenda to Bonniejean Christen-
sen's list appeared in the *Bulletin of Bibliography* for
July-September, 1977, we decided it was unnecessary.)
Publication, however, does not tell the whole story.
Scarcely a scholarly meeting devoted to twentieth-
century literature or science fiction/fantasy/romance
or popular culture does not have at least one paper on
Tolkien, and separate MLA seminars have been devoted
entirely to him at the national convention.

Perhaps nobody could be expected to keep up with all this activity (though Richard West, in his periodical *Orcrist,* makes a commendable attempt). But it seems to us important to try to distinguish those efforts produced by and for Tolkien *fans* from those which have value for serious students (or readers) of literature. This is a distinction which has not always been made, even by Tolkien's American publishers, who in 1974 issued the enormously simple-minded *Tolkien's World* by Randel Helms just two years after publishing Paul Kocher's excellent *Master of Middle-earth.*

Three collections of essays have made varied contributions to the literature. The *Mankato Studies in English* volume (1967) contains ten items, of which eight are rather broad discussions that add little to our understanding or appreciation. The exceptions, both by Kathryn Blackmun ("The Development of Runic and Fëanorian Alphabets for the Transliteration of English" and "Translations from the Elvish"), are highly recommended for anyone interested in such matters, but are too specialized to be reprinted here.

Jared Lobdell's *A Tolkien Compass* (1975) is distinguished chiefly by Tolkien's own "Guide to the Names in *The Lord of the Rings*" for the use of translators. The other ten essays may be generally characterized as offering occasional valuable insights, particularly those by Christensen, West, Huttar, and Dorothy Matthews. None seemed so valuable as to demand reprinting here.

Mark Hillegas's *Shadows of Imagination* (1976) had four essays on Tolkien, of which three are worthy of attention: one by Charles Moorman, one by Gunnar Urang, and one by Daniel Hughes. Moorman was represented in our first collection by a chapter from his *Precincts of Felicity,* and we felt that this later essay, which concerns C. S. Lewis as well as Tolkien, would not be appropriate for us. Urang's contribution is a chapter from his *Shadows of Heaven* (Philadelphia, 1971), "Tolkien's Fantasy: The Phenomenology of Hope"; we felt that the positive value of its insights did not justify a second reprinting of an essay that long. As for the original Hughes piece, it is so good that we felt compelled to include it.

Among books on Tolkien that, with the Helms volume, fairly clearly fall into the category of fan fluff are

William Ready's *The Tolkien Relation* (1968) and Lin
Carter's *Tolkien: A Look behind The Lord of the Rings*
(1969). It is difficult to imagine publishers justify-
ing the issue of three comparable books of (loosely defined) literary criticism on any other author or subject
than Tolkien. One might reasonably assume that those
three were motivated by a common desire to cash in on
the cultic phenomena, but the same should not be said
for Clyde S. Kilby's *Tolkien and the Silmarillion* (Whea-
ton, Ill., 1976), though its value is equally slight.

Kilby, who also contributed the fourth Tolkien essay
to the Hillegas collection, seems to have had two distinct impulses behind his little book. One is the wish
to celebrate his own relationship with Tolkien, for
which he can hardly be blamed; perhaps every Tolkien fan
will be indulgent on this count. The other is to serve
as Tolkien's Christian apologist, describing him as a
"staunchly conservative Tridentine Roman Catholic" who
had "a special reverence for the Virgin Mary" (p. 53).
Kilby asserts, on the basis of "evidence" which he neither cites nor reveals, that Tolkien "intended a final
glorious eventuality similar to the one described in the
Book of Revelation," and so Kilby as would-be prophet
foresaw an end to the "ubiquitous evil of such as Morgoth and Sauron" along with, among other wonders, "the
lands lying under the waves lifted up, the Silmarils recovered, Eärendil returned to the earth, the Two Trees
rekindled...the dead...raised and the original purposes
of Eru executed" (pp. 64-65).

All this proceeds from the argument that "Tolkien
was too pronounced a believer in Christ as the Sovereign
Ruler who was to come" *not* to add all this. Such reasoning takes Kilby's work beyond the bounds of literary
criticism. The eschatological glimpses in *The Silmarillion* only serve to put into perspective the proportion-
ally minute use of explicitly Christian mythology in
Tolkien's subcreation. This is neither to disparage
Kilby's faith nor to discredit Tolkien's, which admit-
tedly could be inferred from the rare clues in the trilogy. The problem is that, while a congenial Christianity may explain some readers' affinity for Tolkien's
fiction, a projection of the religion that stands behind
the writer provides little illumination of the work itself, and may very often mislead.

There are five books on Tolkien that are worth serious attention by readers. Probably most obvious is
Humphrey Carpenter's biography (1977), a thorough, af-
fectionate, but judicious volume. By not presuming to
analyze the Tolkien *opera,* Carpenter has provided more
insights to the works than he might have had he indulged
in detailed critical exegesis. There will no doubt be
further biographical attention to Tolkien, but at best
Carpenter's book will be joined rather than replaced.

From Australia comes J. S. Ryan's *Tolkien: Cult or
Culture?* (Armidale, N.S.W., 1969), an interesting col-
lage, including essays by other hands as separate chapters. Not readily available in this country, the book,
despite its title and uneven quality, deserves consider-
ation. We include here a more fully developed version
of one of the chapters by Ryan.

The essays by Catharine Stimpson in the Columbia
Essays on Modern Writers (1969) and Robley Evans in the
Writers for the 70's series (1972) may be usefully considered together. Both confront the issue of popular
appeal, with quite different results. Stimpson comes
down quite solidly against Tolkien, suggesting that
unlike Joyce's energy which forged "borrowed elements
together to make his work transcendent," Tolkien's
"earnest vision seems syncretic, his structure a col-
lage, and his feeling antiquarian." Her dubious implicit definition of "modern" objects to the "many, many
echoes" in *The Lord of the Rings.* Evans, on the other
hand, seems pleased to discover echoes, assuming that
there is a place in the 1970s and beyond for writers
who evoke associations with classical, medieval, Renaissance, and romantic traditions, not to mention the popular narrative art of the Victorian period.

Stimpson's "modernist" position leads inevitably to
a rejection of Tolkien on political grounds: "Tolkien's
stubborn, self-deluding conservatism also demands that
we respect families and dynasties. The personal consequence? Chromosomes are destiny. The political consequence? Hereditary power. The social consequence? A
rigid class system" (p. 13). Worse, "Tolkien is irrita-
tingly, blandly, traditionally masculine" (p. 18) with
an attitude toward sex that is "a little childish, a
little nasty, and evasive" (p. 20). Evans, who does not
feel called upon to *vote* for Tolkien, and who may share

Stimpson's anticlassist, antisexist, antiageist, anti-
traditionalist attitudes for all we know, nevertheless
finds in *The Lord of the Rings* bases for continued appeal to contemporary audiences.

The trouble with this point counterpoint is rhetorical imbalance. For the purposes of literary judgment,
Stimpson operates from a crippling set of political bi-
ases. But next to Evans's propriety her one-liners are
irresistible. "Tolkien is bogus; bogus, prolix, and
sentimental. His popularization of the past is a comic
strip for grown-ups. *The Lord of the Rings* is almost as
colorful and easy as *Captain Marvel*. That easiness is
perhaps the source of Tolkien's appeal. His intellectual, emotional, and imaginative energies are timid and
jejune" (p. 43). It is hard to gainsay that Tolkien is
"a kindly pediatrician to the soul" (p. 42) and impossible not to smile at "Frodo lives, on borrowed time" (p.
45). For a full and proper response to Stimpson (and
other devaluers of Tolkien), the reader should turn to
Paul Kocher's *Master of Middle-earth* — or perhaps to
Tolkien: New Critical Perspectives.

We begin with Lionel Basney's original essay, which
treats Tolkien's creation of myth and "feigned history"
and incidentally sets aside the cultic distractions of
Middle-earth fandom. Next J. S. Ryan deals with critical principles enunciated by Tolkien at a time when he
was barely beginning *The Lord of the Rings* and shows
that he practiced what he preached. Ryan uses the short
story "Leaf by Niggle" as his example, "an allegory of
...the artist's creative exercise."

The next three essays relate Tolkien's material
in *The Lord of the Rings* to a variety of traditions.
Verlyn Flieger's contribution, adapted from her 1977
Catholic University dissertation, urges the value of
recognizing the medieval heritage of Tolkien's heroes.
Rose Zimbardo's focus is on the structure of the trilogy which she relates to the Renaissance concept of *discordia concors*. Then Daniel Hughes extends the frame
of reference for Tolkien's readers to the high romantic
tradition of Coleridge, Shelley, Wordsworth, Hopkins,
Scott, and Blake.

The essay by Patrick Grant, reprinted from *Cross
Currents*, moves from Blake's vision and the postromantic
tradition of Tolkien and his friends to a careful anal-

ysis of *The Lord of the Rings* in terms of Jungian archetypes. In his analysis Grant comes to terms with the
Christianity implicit in Tolkien's work in a way that
Kilby could not. Then David Jeffrey's original piece
moves through considerations of allegory, allusion, and
pattern (again with an implicit Christianity) to philological and onomastic concerns. The reader will find
examples both challenging and provocative. We next offer the first chapter of Kocher's book, a clear exposi-
tion of how Tolkien's created world can be at the same
time "a world elsewhere" (as Richard Poirier uses the
phrase) and a very real part of our own.

Succeeding essays treat neglected aspects of Tolkien's work. Henry Parks deals with the significance of
Tolkien's criticism, not as a guide to reading his fiction, but in its own right as occupying a central position in contemporary critical thought (inevitably this
means vis-à-vis Northrop Frye); and Lois Kuznets exam-
ines *The Hobbit* as a work in the mainstream of traditional British children's literature.

Finally, we offer contrasting reviews of *The Silmarillion,* both well argued and each representative of
one of the two dominant critical responses the work has
evoked. To Joseph McLellan, its best parts stand up
well under comparisons with Hesiod, *The Iliad, Paradise
Lost,* and Genesis, while to Robert M. Adams it is an
"empty and pompous bore." Perhaps both are right. The
real paradox is that those who are most eagerly drawn
to the book as a major object of their cultic attention
will most easily be put off by its remoteness from *The
Lord of the Rings*.

It was our considered decision not to wait for full
and careful critical analysis of *The Silmarillion* before
offering this collection, for several reasons. First,
Christopher Tolkien promises at least another volume of
material assembled from the fragments of his father's
subcreated world, and we think that it should all be
judged together. We also think that no individual seg-
ment is so significant by itself as to hold up publication, although the metaphor of creation-by-music and the
tale of Túrin Turambar (among other attractive items)
might well elicit valuable exegesis. Finally, we are
ever more firmly convinced that *The Lord of the Rings*
is the creative work most worthy of critical attention,

and the emphasis of our book reflects that conviction.

The publication of *The Silmarillion* should nevertheless stimulate some reexamination of certain critical
issues regarding the trilogy. For example, the question
of the appropriateness of the appendixes at the end of
The Return of the King will have to be reopened. If
they are considered integral parts of the esthetic design of *The Lord of the Rings*, could not much of the assembled lore in *The Silmarillion* also be included? Or
perhaps all the cosmogonical, cosmological, and apocalyptic material that stands behind the great narrative
of the trilogy should be considered to subsume all the
back matter — genealogical, philological, onomastic, and
gazetteerical — in both books.

Certainly a reexamination of Tolkien's style is in
order. As I said in reviewing *The Silmarillion* for the
Washington Star, its style "will stun many, particularly
those who know Tolkien as the author of '*Beowulf:* the
Monsters and the Critics,' still the most lucid and
readable essay in all Old English scholarship. This
book is persistently Biblical. The Book of Numbers
comes most often to mind. And so it is that, beyond all
hope, Christopher son of J. R. R. has brought the new
Tolkien to light in the world of men." The point is
that new attention will be drawn by contrast to those
stylistic aspects of the trilogy that breathe life into
its subcreation: narrative power, droll charm, intricate
playfulness, and physical and psychological detail. All
this is substantially absent from the solemnly sacred
text of *The Silmarillion.*

We have had to make some difficult decisions in
keeping this book to its present size. Basically, we
have been guided by a criterion of broad applicability,
so that some very good but comparatively narrow papers
were omitted. I think particularly of Veronica Ken-
nedy's folkloristic insights and J. Russell Reavers'
"Gandalf as a Bodhissatva." Both, I trust, will be published, as the necessary process of critical elucidation
of a major work of art goes on.

Lionel Basney

MYTH, HISTORY, AND TIME IN 'THE LORD OF THE RINGS'

The Lord of the Rings is the story of a quest, and of a
world in which the quest takes place, a world in which
it can be meaningful. All fiction, in a sense, creates
its own world, in that it is thoroughly intentional;
all the details of the fictional world are chosen. But
few stories create worlds so different from our own as
Tolkien's. Few bother with nonhuman races, extinct
languages, magical powers. Not all fiction, in other
words, is fantasy.

Not all fantasy, moreover, is so successful as Tolkien's at creating a world that seems to possess solidity, orderliness, and integrity as well as vivacity and
color. The reader's sensation in *The Lord of the Rings*
is that he can trust the vision presented — not, of
course, to be more than a vision, but to be wholly coherent and consistent within itself. Once he enters the
"Secondary World," as Tolkien would say, he may trust
the laws of that world to govern all appearances and
events.[1] The narrative unfolds the world to us. But it
also validates it; new characters, events, and topography fulfill, rather than violate, the expectations that
have been raised in our minds.

The central characteristic of Tolkien's work — thus
the one the critic must explain first and most carefully
— is this structural and tonal integrity. It is not
mere thematic unity. Indeed Tolkien tended to reject
most efforts to define the "themes" of his work. Nor is
this integrity simply a matter of the suspense generated
by a well-told story. Though a function of the story,
integrity is not a property of the story alone, but of

the entire project. Tolkien's success depends rather on his project's obedience to certain basic structures and movements on all its levels: plot, fantasy-world, the literary form of the work as a whole. The most comprehensive of these structures are "myth" and "history"; the most general movement, the growth of one into the other. Before substantiating this claim, however, we must develop a series of parallel contrasts that stand behind the dualism of myth and history in the text of *The Lord of the Rings*.

The first of these contrasts affects the work's format as a book. It opposes the "world" Tolkien has invented to the main events narrated by his story. The world, "Middle-earth," exists before and after these events; it is ordered, hierarchical, historical, all but static. The specific occurrence Tolkien narrates — not the whole history of Middle-earth, but a brief, intense incident from that history — is Frodo's quest, a journey, full of chance, disconnected experience, frequent shifts in rhythm, the gradual maturation, under stress, of given qualities good and bad. This second structure is essentially dynamic, motive. From the perspective of Middle-earth as a world, the events of Frodo's journey are seen *sub specie aeternitatis* (in a fictional sense), as a pattern of historical events rescued from time by having been recorded, fitted into the larger pattern of the world's history. For the journey, Middle-earth as a world provides its inalienable conditions, determining, in the most general sense, what can and cannot happen. It also contains the past: the roots of present conflict and the repository of ideals.

Some readers have expressed a critical preference for one of these structures over another. William Ready, for instance, gives his attention to the quest, wishing that Tolkien had not included the appendixes which summarize Middle-earth's genealogical and philological history.[2] But the opposing structures are both necessary. The quest reveals and illuminates the world; the world provides the determining conditions of the quest.

According to Tolkien, moreover, the mock scholarly apparatus which contains Middle-earth's lineaments as a world was conceived before the quest (I,5). *The Lord of the Rings* developed from Tolkien's children's story,

....

The Hobbit (1937), but not directly. What intervened
was an effort to set in order the pre-*Hobbit* past of
Middle-earth by providing philological histories of its
ancient tongues (especially Elvish). In this there was
little narrative invention. Tolkien was only recalled
to narrative by his friends' curiosity about the "present-day" story, the matter of the Ring; then, over a
period of a decade and a half, he composed the six narrative books we now have. By distinguishing between
"ancient history," with its mock philology and imaginary
genealogies, and the *story* of the Ring, Tolkien shows
that the opposition of cosmos and journey has its counterpart in the work's format. In a sense, *The Lord of
the Rings* may be regarded as a descendant of *A Tale of
a Tub* and *Sartor Resartus,* with its combination of narrative and "scholarly" material — introduction, appendixes, index, maps, and the pretense of translation
from older literatures. Tolkien and Swift are different
largely in mood. Swift was intent on multiple satire.
Tolkien's "scholarship" validates and supports his
story, giving it a context, the "Secondary World," to
inhabit.

Two further contrasts between the static and the
dynamic are to be found in the narrative itself. The
first works as a fundamental organizing device of Tolkien's plot: movement versus tableau. The flight to
Rivendell versus the enclosed, comfortable scenes of
Bree and the Shire; Rivendell itself versus the journey
to Moria; Lothlórien, the still center of Middle-earth,
with its memory of the Elder Days, versus the turmoil of
war in Rohan and Gondor. Dominating the story's climax
is the tableau of the serene White Tower versus the
nightmarish creeping trek of Sam and Frodo through Mordor. Tolkien varies this device as a way of emphasizing
distance and loneliness: Pippin in Gondor thinks of Sam
and Frodo. The device is further, but logically, extended to include a contrast between a character's immediate effort and his ultimate vision. In the absence
from Middle-earth of explicitly noumenal values, this
vision must usually be phenomenal and spatial: Aragorn
carries with him the vision of Lórien. Struggling in
Mordor's desolation, Sam thinks of the Shire, which
means to him all the things he is ready to sacrifice
himself for: home, comfort, the earth's fruitfulness,
the hobbits' secure bourgeois contentment.

The second plot distinction leads us near our larger dualism. Tolkien makes a distinction between action and lore, between the existential and the literal, and the distinction is an essential component of the story. Part of the effort against Sauron, a part that is almost exclusively Gandalf's responsibility, is the identification of the One Ring. To assemble its history, to link it with "Isildur's Bane" and the Gladden Fields, Gandalf exercises what is essentially historical research; this carries him from hearsay and legend to the formal archives of Minas Tirith. Without this coherent lore, the Ring, unrecognized, would have been calamitously easy for Sauron to recover.

The importance of "lore" in Middle-earth is not only utilitarian. It is valued for itself. Further, we find it undergoing a definite evolution. During the time covered by Tolkien's narrative, the fundamentally oral-mythical traditions of Rohan and Rivendell are in the process of being written down, of assuming specifically literary form. This process derives from an impulse belonging primarily to hobbits, whose tidy minds demand comfortable, transparent orders and accurate records. (It is significant that hobbits are the only race in Middle-earth to construct museums. This indicates the relatively low-key, companionable though precise reminiscence which fills the same demand in the Shire that epic song fills in Rohan.)

But the immediate stimulus of the process is the War of the Ring, which brings the hobbits out of xenophobic isolation and makes them the historians of the reestablished Kingdom. The ancient legend which gets written down is that most closely associated with the War. Bilbo, for instance, composes creditable poetry about the Elder Days. This is appreciated, in the Rivendell manner, through communal recitation. But he also works at setting in order the written account of his travels, which later becomes, with Frodo's crucial additions, the core of the Ring's official history. This history is finally completed by the hobbits, though it is glossed and edited as well in Gondor (I,23-25).

A different stage in the progression from legend to history appears in Rohan. Midway between the hobbits' bourgeois democracy and the aboriginal state of the "wild men," the Rohirrim live in a heroic honor-culture where manhood means military prowess and knowledge the

"ancient lay." Their relatively primitive historical
consciousness is at root identical with their limited
insight in the scope of Middle-earth. Of Lórien they
know only nursery tales about Galadriel, whom they think
a sorceress. Ignorant of Sauron or magic seeing stones,
Rohan sees Saruman and Gondor simply as military enemy
and ally. Though they regard themselves as ancient, the
Rohirrim are in fact perilously young and naïve; their
limited awareness defines, and is defined by, their lack
of comprehensive "lore," their estrangement from the
mythical springs of ancient history at Rivendell and
Lórien.

The hobbits' transformation of oral-mythical legend
into formal history is the most literary example of the
story's "realization" of myth. But it is not the only
example. The plot also "realizes" the cultural myths of
its races, by matching events with their mythical equiv-
alents, allowing the legend to be fulfilled by actual
enactment in the plot. Because of their relative igno-
rance, the Rohirrim are the prototype of a people seeing
its legends and nursery rhymes come to actual life. But
others have the same experience. Frodo's quest is a
birth into knowledge for the hobbits who accompany him.
Moreover, the races who encounter the hobbits find their
appearance a challenge to credulity and scepticism. The
hobbits seem literally a myth come to life, to living
fact.

The general pattern of this repeated incarnation is
as follows: an individual character, often on his home
ground and thus confident of his ability to judge rightly, suddenly recognizes that some reality of which he
had known only in legend now faces him in broad daylight, or is attested to by authority he cannot gainsay.
The character's response is normally a blend of surprise, assent, and wonder. For the reality he confronts
does not thereby lose its mythical fascination. Rather
the myth merges with experience, or into experience, its
wonder intact, but having gained empirical solidity.

This experience of recognition occurs in pure form
at least fifteen times in the trilogy. It is worth
specifying these, to indicate their variety, and also
to suggest their importance to the larger pattern of
events. First are the three instances of characters'
encountering hobbits: Haldir, an elf (I,357); Éothain in

Rohan (II,37); Beregond in Minas Tirith (III,33). The
hobbits encounter two specifically legendary beings:
Pippin comes across the trolls of Bilbo's tale (I,218);
Sam sees an oliphaunt (II,255,270). Boromir learns from
Elrond about the Ring's fate, about which Gondor's tales
have only hinted (I,256); he also hears from Celeborn
about ents (I,390). With him in this are Aragorn and
Legolas, who hear more particulars from Gandalf (II,
102). Gandalf also tells Gimli of the Endless Stair,
which he has visited (II,105). Several encounters are
closely related to the War itself. Éomer meets Aragorn
and his identifying sword, and hears from the three com-
panions about the reality of Galadriel (II,35-36). Like
his brother, Faramir encounters the Ring (II,289), and
later tells Denethor of the halflings "that I have seen
walking out of northern legends" (III,84). The men of
Lossarnach and Rohan march to battle in Mordor, which
had been only a legend to them (III,162). Finally, Im-
rahil's family story about elf-ancestry is confirmed by
Legolas, who can see it in him (III,148). In each case
some intimation of hobbits, ents, and so on, had been
given by a familiar story: the story, once ignored or
disbelieved, turns out to be a version of sober fact.

   "Dreams and legends," says Éomer, "spring to life
out of the grass" (II,36). C. S. Lewis commented that
Éomer's distinction between legend and reality was
"rash."[3] But if this distinction were less clear to the
peoples of Middle-earth, their shock and wonder would
also be less. The experience of myth-realization is to
Éomer the harbinger of a new and special era, a time in
which ultimate battles must be fought. Nor does the experience take place indiscriminately. It generally
opens to certain characters the existence of others of
whom we have already been aware; and, in any case, it
must obey the ontological limits of Middle-earth as a
world. Plainly, many legends remain legends; and
Tolkien is selective on principle. It is through the
transformation of certain myths into experience that the
free peoples recognize each other, and their common destiny and enemy. Their common knowledge becomes an active bond among them. It is as if their alliance had
been latent in cultural and racial myth, awaiting the
special events which actualize it and bring it into dynamic focus.

It should be plain where our initially structural dualism is leading us. The movement from legend to experience, from "imaginary" to "real" (though even the real is fictive), extends inevitably to a conception of time, one of the two which jointly govern Middle-earth. These two conceptions spring from opposing *ethoi*. The less important is pagan, "northern," its paradigm *Beowulf;* its corresponding time pattern is cyclical and deterministic, seeing human civilization as an effort to buy time from forces of evil which always rise after defeat to be met again.[4] We glimpse this *ethos* in Gandalf's counsel that Frodo should concern himself with the affairs of his time, and that the shadow of which Sauron is only a manifestation can never be fully destroyed (I,60).

To this pagan pattern the unfolding, evolving movement which realizes legend is clearly opposed. The *ethos* here is Judeo-Christian; its corresponding notion is the "fullness of time," the progressive blossoming of mysterious intent that produces a necessary answer at the instant it is needed. There is, indeed, little messianism in Tolkien's plan. It seems to Frodo that he is singled out by chance. But the time pattern of messianic promise is essential: the gradual unfolding of mythical possibilities, or of possibilities grasped only by myth, into plain reality. This revelation obeys the tempo of its time. We see Middle-earth in a state of crisis. Each day summons its myth "out of the grasses." But, as Gandalf's painful research into the Ring's course from Isildur to Frodo makes plain, the progress of time toward its realizing moment has never stopped; it has only been ignored, or preserved in the amber of legend.

Thus the main characters of *The Lord of the Rings* sense that they are living in a time of prophecy-fulfillment. These are the days when "it has come to pass, which was spoken of." Tolkien calls them the "Great Years" at the close of the Third Age (III,372). The Fourth Age opens with the passing of Elrond Halfelven across the sea, and the final disappearance from Middle-earth of all who had had direct dealings with the Ring (III,363,378). This period is also the transition from the "Elder Days" to the age of men (i.e., our age). Though in the prologue to *The Lord of the Rings* (I,10)

Tolkien suggests that hobbits still inhabit the world, the passing of the Elder Days effectively closes the day of fantasy, and we find ourselves at the dawn of man's hegemony. The unfolding of Tolkien's time scheme brings him inevitably from the world of myth to that of human history. The nonhuman "speaking peoples" pass to the West, die, or retreat into silence, and the story ends when all the "faerie" potentials of Tolkien's plan have been, or are about to be, exhausted.

At the trilogy's end, therefore, we are in some sense in the present-day world. We are, at least, out of the world of faerie. Tolkien makes no effort to merge the Fourth Age with any recognizable epoch of human record. But the *sine qua non* of faerie has been lost: the opportunity for contact between man and the other beings and traditions.[5] It is thus perfectly logical that after completing *The Lord of the Rings* Tolkien returned to his earlier preoccupation, the history of former ages. The *Silmarillion,* on which he worked sporadically in the years before his death, was to carry us back to the Elder times, the ages which are merely legend even to Aragorn. It is clear that Tolkien had no more to say of the Fourth Age. The proper evolution of its fantasy time carries Middle-earth from the far past, to which memory can penetrate only by means of imagination, of myth, to the virtual present, after the possibility of the fantasy experience has disappeared along with the faerie races.

The agency of this evolution is never defined. The elves' desire to pass to the West obeys a sort of paradisal nostalgia that is their racial possession and, in a sense, their identity. But it is consequently confined to them. Nor are the historical "ages" in any way causal. They end, generally, with a defeat of the Shadow and a new lease on life for Middle-earth's population. But what determines the make-up of this population, or the ways in which it seems unavoidably to change, Tolkien does not specify. The "West" holds both purpose and power; it is, however, up to the races of Middle-earth to attend to their own business. Gandalf tells Frodo that he was *"meant"* to receive and own the Ring (I,65) — in which case some of the events in the ensuing narrative were also "meant." But the agency can be no clearer.

This causal vagueness is essential, I think, because it inhibits our critical impulse to read some abstract dogma into Tolkien's story. Tolkien himself insisted that he was not writing allegory (I,7); and the conflicting *ethoi* in Middle-earth's time patterns should warn us off. The movement from past to present obeys a definite, ingrained teleology, but this is the urge of Tolkien's fictional mode and not of a dictating creed. It is a movement from myth to history, from the mythical world communicated by imagination to the historical record embodied in Tolkien's charts, tables, and glosses.

Tolkien's enigmatic insistence that in *The Lord of the Rings* he was writing "history" (I,7) becomes clearer in the light of this overall movement. For the essential development of Tolkien's narrative is the conversion of myth or legend into history, that is, into the real and calculable: from the vague prophecies of communal tradition, to the halflings "walking out of legend" into broad daylight, to the meticulous records of the hobbit historians. The culminating step of this process is Tolkien's own act of composition. Middle-earth's Fourth Age has no discernible connection with human history, as we have said; on the contrary, Middle-earth's "present" is in Tolkien's writing, his pretense of translation from recovered old-language histories, his careful setting in order of the ancient evidence. This is what the nature of his world demands. One of Middle-earth's governing cosmic conditions is the growth of legend into history. And Tolkien's work is the final reduction of the Elder Days into present-day form. As long as the hobbits were, so to speak, elaborating their history, Middle-earth's story (and nature) remained fluid. But with Tolkien's act of composition, this potential is actualized, fixed, final, entire. In *The Lord of the Rings,* Tolkien at once imagines and fulfills the historical development of his world.

For his work, therefore, history is the mode of fixed and completed reality, existence rescued from time and adumbrated in logic. Tolkien could not have written the history of the Ring until the characters and events associated with it — until its world — had become "historical," that is, irredeemably past. The way fantasy is exhausted at the close of the Third Age makes Tolkien's history possible. No further development of the

seminal myth could be expected. On the other hand, the
Ring's affairs may be said to comprise history only in
the act of Tolkien's writing. Only in the fixed, intentional record which is his narrative is his fantasy
fixed, specified, made real. By telling his story, Tolkien has realized his myth, and also the myths his mythical characters possess and create.

The link between the "past" of Middle-earth and
Tolkien's work is his pretense of scholarship. The
imagined transcription and translation of materials from
hobbit manuscripts — the very tables and charts which
some readers find tiresome — make the integrity of Tolkien's work possible. Because he treats his work not as
deliberate fiction — allegory, which depends for validity on something truer than itself — but as history, his
invented world can itself claim historical solidity and
independence. It determines and fulfills its own historical conditions. One of these conditions, moreover,
is our central dualism, which can be seen on all levels
of the work: the dualism of myth (or story) and history
(or fact), along with the realization of the first in
the second.

The crucial difference between the realization of
myth within Tolkien's narrative and outside it should
also be clear. For Middle-earth's inhabitants, myth
becomes history by way of experience. For us, myth becomes experience only by way of Tolkien's history. The
culturally juvenile impulse to treat Middle-earth as
having other than literary existence — other than a
feigned history — stems from the failure to remember
that Middle-earth exists only in words, in the chosen
details of Tolkien's narrative, to which nothing can be
added. By inventing Middle-earth, Tolkien also fixed it
beyond change. The dynamism of myth and history is only
an inner dynamism, which nevertheless explains some of
the story's narrative interest. It also explains part
of the "integrity" of Middle-earth: our sense that Tolkien's manner of presenting his invention is wholly at
one with its nature.

Tolkien liked to talk of fantasy as an unfolding of
the potentials of God's creation, an addition to the
actual cosmos.[6] Middle-earth too is a kind of cosmos;
but we can make no additions to it. It unfolds no further than the text. We are not mistaken, however, if

we feel that Middle-earth does "unfold" within its own boundaries. Its very nature as a world is to develop and grow, particularly to develop realities out of apparent fiction. Like those of the real world, Middle-earth's values and structure are revealed dynamically, in the course of a process of development which is also a growth of perception. As readers we observe this process affecting the lives and destinies of Tolkien's characters. But it affects as well the very form of the work we are reading and, thus, the kind of reading we do. We too experience the gradual realization of imagined beings and events. We too, after our fashion, meet halflings "walking out of legend."

Notes

1. See "On Fairy-Stories," esp. p. 37.   2. William Ready, *The Tolkien Relation* (Chicago, 1968), pp. 6, 44, 83.   3. Lewis, "The Dethronement of Power," in *T & C,* p. 15.   4. Ready, p. 4 and passim.   5. See "On Fairy-Stories," passim.
    6. Ibid., p. 73.

J. S. Ryan

FOLKTALE, FAIRY TALE, AND THE CREATION OF A STORY

In a form more compact than that of Williams, and with a simpler, more consistently presented philosophy than that of C. S. Lewis, Tolkien has explained for us his views of the function of myth. At the same time he has shown himself the best critic of his own major work[1] — a feat all the more illuminating of his consistency of thought when we realize that his theories appear to have been fully evolved when he had just begun the trilogy; original versions of his "On Fairy-Stories" and "Leaf by Niggle" were "written in the same period (1938-1939), when *The Lord of the Rings* was beginning to unroll itself and to unfold prospects of labour in yet unknown country."[2]

Although they are not as specific as one might like, it is best to note first the various comments Tolkien made in 1936 when he was lecturing on *Beowulf*, in a paper now widely recognized as a turning point in *Beowulf* criticism, stressing as it did the tragedy of the human condition and showing how that tragedy is set forth in artistic terms as "a balance of ends and beginnings," "the moving contrast of youth and age," with the monsters, embodying the forces of evil and chaos, appropriately placed in the center of the poem. In his remarks Tolkien indicates that he is in sympathy with the poet for using afresh ancient and largely traditional material and for giving something nearer to mythical allegory than the folktale. He warns that formal intellectual snobbishness should not blind us to this:

> I will not...attempt at length a defence of the
> mythical mode of imagination.... Folk-tales...do
> often contain much that is far more powerful, and

that cannot be sharply separated from myth...capable
in poetic hands of...becoming largely significant —
as a whole, accepted unanalysed. The significance
of a myth is not easily to be pinned on paper by an-
alytical reasoning. It is at its best when it is
presented by a poet who feels rather than makes explicit what his theme portends: who presents it incarnate in the world of history and geography...;
myth is alive at once and in all its parts, and
dies before it can be dissected. It is possible, I
think, to be moved by the power of myth and yet to
misunderstand the sensation,...[to] refuse to admit
that there can be an interest for *us*...in ogres and
dragons.[3]

He goes on to stress the impact of *draconitas,* lust for
power over possessions and people, a large symbolism of
malice, greed, and destruction, here walking in history
and incarnate in time, and he underscores the inevitable
overthrow of man in Time, for *líf is lǽne,* a theme
which, in its deadly seriousness, begets the dignity of
tone. He notes that the poem is by a great Christian
just over the threshold of religious change, who has the
uplifting hope which was denied his heroic ancestors.
    Interestingly, Tolkien regrets that we do not know
more "about pre-Christian English mythology" (p. 70), a
gap which, it has often been felt, this scholar has been
concerned to fill in his own creative writings. He is
also here determined to stress the impact of the story
from its cosmic dimension: "It is just because the main
foes in *Beowulf* are inhuman that the story is larger and
more significant.... It glimpses the cosmic and moves
with the thought of all men concerning the fate of human
life and efforts; it stands amid but above the petty
wars of princes, and surpasses the dates and limits of
historical periods.... During its process we look down
as if from a visionary height upon the house of man in
the valley of the world" (pp. 87f.). In his conclusion
Tolkien notes that the poet is concerned to use materials then plentiful but from a day already passing,
a time now for ever vanished; using them for a new
purpose, with a wider sweep of the imagination, and
achieving a peculiar solemnity so that for all those of
northern races "it must ever call with a profound appeal
— until the dragon comes" (p. 88).

As his better-known minor writings indicate,[4] Tolkien's imagination was nourished on the materials of Old Norse and Old English literature, and on certain other texts from the Middle English period; therefore, it comes as no surprise to find that the strands and themes that are woven into the fabric of the major works are rich in Germanic associations. Yet early indications of certain concepts (e.g., that both in process and in nature man's imagination is like a tree) seem to have been overlooked. His 1926 essay in *The Year's Work in English Studies* ended this way: "This study...is fired by the two emotions, love of the land of England and the allurement of the riddle of the past, that never cease to carry men through amazing...labours to the recapturing of fitful and tantalizing glimpses in the dark — 'Floreant Philologica et Archaeologica.'"[5] In 1927, he began his survey with lines which are a startling anticipation of "Leaf by Niggle," as well as of Aragorn and others in the woods of Lothlórien. Interestingly, they echo Dante and Frazer's *The Golden Bough:* "It is merry in summer when 'shaws be sheen and shrads full fair and leaves both large and long.' Walking in that wood is full of solace. Its leaves require no reading. There is another and a denser wood where some are obliged to walk instead, where saws are wise and screeds are thick and the leaves too large and long. These leaves we must read (more or less), hapless vicarious readers, and not all we read is solace."[6]

Yet it was the need to clarify his own comments on *Beowulf* about "the mythical mode of imagination" which may be assumed to have prompted the essay wherein he is concerned to describe the genre, fairy tale, in a way that does not relate well to many examples of the form, but which does apply very closely to his own writing (and is accepted by Lewis who uses it, without acknowledgment, when defending his friend's three volumes).[7] While it is possible to trace the lines of Tolkien's thought back through Chesterton's "The Ethics of Elfland,"[8] and earlier to George Macdonald's "Imagination, Its Functions and Its Culture,"[9] and thence to Coleridge, in the *Biographia Literaria,* it will be enough here to analyze what is a substantially new piece of work which goes much further than its predecessors and argues its case with greater cogency and fuller development than they.

While both Chesterton and Tolkien are pointedly un-
concerned about the origin of the fairy tale, they are
alike attentive to its meaning and purpose. Chesterton
had become disillusioned about "practical politics" but
was committed to "vision," "ordinary things" and "the
sense of the miracle of humanity." "Ordinary things are
more valuable than extraordinary things.... Man is something more awful than men.... The mere man on two legs,
as such, should be felt as something more heart-breaking
than any music" (pp. 67-68). He goes on to stress that
"a legend...ought to be treated more respectfully than
a book of history"; "tradition means giving votes to the
most obscure of all classes, our ancestors"; "I would
always trust the old wives' fables against the old
maids' facts"; "Fairyland is nothing but the sunny country of common sense"; "the test of fairyland...is the
test of imagination"; "we all like astonishing tales because they touch the nerve of the ancient instinct of
astonishment"; or "wonder has a positive element of
praise."

Tolkien in "On Fairy-Stories" finds that no definition of them can be arrived at on historical grounds,
and it must rather come from "Faërie," "the realm or
state in which fairies have their being," "the Perilous
Realm itself" which holds "the seas, the sun, the moon,
the sky, and the earth, and all the things that are in
it; tree and bird, water and stone, wine and bread, and
ourselves, mortal men, when we are enchanted" (p. 9).

Further, most good "fairy-stories" are about the
aventures of men in that realm. Perhaps the best translation of "Faërie" is Magic "of a peculiar mood and
power" which operates to give us "the enchantment of
distance," and "the satisfaction of certain primordial
human communion with other living things" (p. 13).

The trilogy in its story is full of echoes of the
dim past, the earlier ages and the ancient forces, and
makes much use of borrowing in time. As is stated early
on, "we stand outside our own time, outside Time itself,
maybe." As well as "opening a door onto other time,"
there the language of the trees is a function of the
story, as are the alien tongues of birds and horses,
while the reader, through the hobbits, is able to communicate with many different rational species, from the
orcs and trolls, and eagles and horses, to the elves

and the High Elves who do not normally commune in words.

All of these processes satisfy the primal desire, of "imagined wonder," which emotion we experience vicariously through the hobbits, as they behold with "wonder" the variety of Middle-earth: Goldberry (I,134); the "silence of the heavens" (I,14); or Strider, as one of the line of the old kings (I,233). Throughout the trilogy we see people bigger than we, existing in a world filled with marvels, both horrifying and beautiful, so that, like the hobbits, we can only gaze with wonder. The men of Gondor marvel at the races of hobbits and dwarves, while the elves themselves have this attitude towards Númenor and the Far West.

In his section on the fairy story's origins, Tolkien acknowledges the validity of the investigation of story elements as an exercise for folklorists, but stresses that "it is precisely the colouring, the atmosphere, the unclassifiable individual details of a story, and above all the general purport that informs with life the undissected bones of the plot, that really count" (pp. 18-19).

In words that both recall his comments on philology cited above and anticipate much later writing, he links several of his own yearnings: "Of course, I do not deny, for I feel strongly, the fascination of the desire to unravel the intricately knotted and ramified history of the branches on the Tree of Tales. It is closely connected with the philologists' study of the tangled skein of Language, of which I know some small pieces" (p. 19). In a change of symbol he argues that the reader should be content with the "soup" as presented, or "the story as it is served up by its author or teller," and not with the bones that went into the mix. [10]

In the making of the fairy story he sees three important ingredients — *invention, inheritance,* and *diffusion.* By the first he probably means collecting knowns in medieval fashion, while the second is "borrowing in time," and the third "borrowing in space," usually from another inventor. At the center is an inventive mind, the nature of which Tolkien (in a manner similar to that of Owen Barfield), [11] would explore. This leads to his analysis of the creative imagination, a theory that utilizes and goes beyond Coleridge's use of Platonic concepts to an implicitly Christian romanti-

cism. "Faërie" is a product of the "esemplastic imagination" of the Secondary World, and this "Secondary
Belief" is much more than the "willing suspension of
disbelief."

Folktales, like all cosmologies, were once myths, or
allegories "of the greater elemental...processes of nature" and only gradually became localized and humanized.
Tolkien disagrees with the view of his friend Christopher Dawson (1889-1970) that they were once separate.[12]
Indeed he stresses that they always were together
"there, in the Cauldron of Story, waiting for the great
figures of Myth and History, and for the yet nameless He
or She, waiting for the moment when they are cast into
the simmering stew" (p. 29). After considering History
and Myth, and the power of many stories which "open a
door on Other Time," he draws attention to the taboos
in stories, and has this to say of tales that are good
enough: "What really happens is that the story-maker
proves a successful 'sub-creator.' He makes a Secondary
World which your mind can enter. Inside it, what he relates is 'true': it accords with the laws of that world.
You therefore believe it, while you are, as it were, inside. The moment disbelief arises, the spell is broken;
the magic, or rather, art, has failed. You are then out
in the Primary World again, looking at the little abor-
tive Secondary World from outside" (p. 37). This is the
distinction between the outer, objective, or Primary
World and the inner world of myth, the Secondary World
produced by the "sub-creator." Tolkien in writing the
trilogy has imaged an entire world and told the story of
certain events which took place during its imagined history.

He is also concerned to underscore in stories the
element of desire. From the tales he read as a child,
he says, came a "wholly unsatisfied desire to shoot well
with a bow" and "glimpses of an archaic mode of life,
and, above all, forests." His taste for these stories,
he tells us, was "wakened by philology...and quickened
to full life by war."

Later, when commenting on the difficulties of being
a successful subcreator, he notes the difficulties involved in commanding Secondary Belief and comments that
few attempt such difficult tasks: "But when they are
attempted and in any degree accomplished then we have

a rare achievement of Art: indeed narrative art, story-
making in its primary and most potent mode" (p. 49).
It is just this craft and fusion, it may be contended,
which produces the peculiar power of *The Lord of the
Rings*.

Coleridge always appealed to Tolkien, and the *Biographia Literaria* was much discussed in various Oxford
groups. Indeed, an early paper of Tolkien's[13] influenced a paper by L. A. Willoughby on Coleridge as philologist:

> He...even thought, for a moment, of turning to
> philology as his profession.... His linguistic
> inquiries took on a psychological bent.... His ap-
> proach was philosophical, aesthetic, religious, and
> only rarely philological in the stricter sense....
> His linguistic observations and suggestions bear
> witness to the sharpness of his intellect and the
> penetration of his intuition. He showed particular
> insight in the cultural aspects of language and a
> keen sense of aesthetic values. But his chief
> strength was the way in which linguistic training
> was put in the service of literary criticism.[14]

The influence of Coleridge is to be found in Tolkien's
discussion of the concept of the creative imagination.
Finding a need for a term other than Fancy "which shall
embrace both the Sub-creative Art in itself and a quality of strangeness and wonder in the Expression...a
quality essential to fairy-story," he proposed "to use
Fantasy for this purpose" (p. 47). In this mode, the
images are of things not of the primary world, but possessed of "arresting strangeness," and the attack on
them is that they are "Dreaming" in which, as Tolkien
admits, "there is no Art," or like Drama which "is
naturally hostile to Fantasy" and which "has, of its
very nature, already attempted a kind of bogus, or shall
I say at least substitute magic.... For this precise
reason — that the characters, and even the scenes [are]
not imagined but actually beheld — Drama is...an art
fundamentally different from narrative art" (p. 51).

Fantasy is an acceptable term to Tolkien for he is
concerned to stress the peculiar ingredients which invented stories offer more fully than "adult" naturalistic ones do: Fantasy, Recovery, Escape, and Consolation.

Needing a new term to express both "Sub-creative Art"
and "a quality of strangeness and wonder," he used Fantasy (in a thesis more elegant than Chesterton's): "We
all like astonishing tales because they touch the nerve
of the ancient instinct of astonishment" (*Orthodoxy*, p.
80). His conclusion suggests a motive for this urge in
men, which he likens to the imagining of gods: "Fantasy
remains a human right: we make in our measure and in our
derivative mode, because we are made: and not only made,
but made in the image and likeness of a Maker" (p. 55).
Recovery, which includes return and renewal of health,
is a "regaining of a clear view." It is a means of
"seeing things as we are (or were) meant to see them."
For although all things once attracted us, "we locked
them in our hoard, acquired them, and acquiring ceased
to look at them." Seeing them only in relation to ourselves, we lose sight of their true nature, but by Recovery we attain again, "dangerous and potent...free and
wild," a fresher and a brighter vision.

As Lewis observed, the method has been used in the
trilogy to considerable effect:

> The value of the myth is that it takes all the
> things we know and restores to them the rich sig-
> nificance which has been hidden by "the veil of
> familiarity."... If you are tired of the real land-
> scape, look at it in a mirror. By putting bread,
> gold, horse, apple, or the very roads into a myth,
> we do not retreat from reality: we rediscover it.
> As long as the story lingers in our mind, the real
> things are more themselves. This book applies the
> treatment not only to bread or apple, but to good
> and evil, to our endless perils, our anguish, and
> our joys. By dipping them in myth we see them more
> clearly.[15]

One might add that the method had been applied to hospi-
tality and courtesy, friendship and heroism, the opera-
tions of greed and the inexorable movement of time —
from the passage of seasons, marked by "holiday and
dancing in the Party Field" (III,390), to "mortal sum-
mers that flicker and pass upon this Middle-earth" (III,
303).

Closely related to Recovery is Escape, the positive,
even heroic, process of getting away from ordinary and
drab surroundings, which is, in effect, "the Escape of

the Prisoner." As Tolkien says, "The world outside has
not become less real because the prisoner cannot see
it."[16] He answers one of the common critical charges
against fantasy when he asks why a man should be scorned
for thinking of topics other than prisons, that is, for
transcending the limits of the actual world. He escapes
the world because he will not accept it; his action
(like any Chestertonian hero's) is rebellion, compounded
of "Disgust, Anger, Condemnation and Revolt." It is a
response to the distortion that leads us to say "How
real, how startlingly alive is a factory chimney compared with an elm-tree." The need for rebellion to
restore one's perspective is well illustrated in the
"scouring of the Shire," where the returning hobbits
find a wilderness of hideous buildings, including just
such a chimney stack. Having come "back again"[17] from
a world where they have gained in moral fiber, they
proceed to set the Shire to rights by first fighting
and routing their enemies and then rebuilding and re-
planting the devastated areas. The lesson of the value
in Escape does not need underscoring; in the trilogy it
is seen in action, in the revitalizing of Minas Tirith,
the rousing of Théoden, and the scouring of Orthanc, and
above all, in the destruction of the Ring, the actuality
of Evil.

The vital element in Escape, however, is Consolation, the consolation of the happy ending, the eucatastrophe, which, by its very fantastic quality, the fairy
story affords as solace for the evils of the world. The
eucatastrophe is the opposite of tragedy, and in its
sudden joyous "turn" gives "a sudden and miraculous
grace: never to be counted on to recur. It does not
deny the existence of *dyscatastrophe,* of sorrow and
failure; the possibility of these is necessary to the
joy of deliverance" (p. 68). Sorrow and evil can be as
keenly felt as in any other literary form and perhaps
more, because of the clear outline of the fairy story;
however "[Fairy story] denies...universal final defeat
and in so far is *evangelium,* giving a fleeting glimpse
of Joy, Joy beyond the walls of the world, poignant as
grief" (p. 68). And so it is that, by means of its
eucatastrophe, fairy story gives the reader a lifting
of the heart, "a piercing glimpse of joy [that] passes
outside the frame, rends indeed the very web of story"
(p. 70).

The relevance of the fairy story to reality lies in the "sudden glimpse of the underlying reality or truth," an "*evangelium* in the real world." This is what the fairy story offers to Tolkien and to other Christians. The Christian view of the happy ending of the world is significantly reflected in the fairy story. For Tolkien (who specifically states his faith), Christianity is a matter of historical fact and a philosophical interpretation of the universe as well as a religion. It is also the archetypal myth of which all others are confused images. "The Birth of Christ is the eucatastrophe of Man's history. The Resurrection is the eucatastrophe of the story of the Incarnation" (p. 72).

The conclusion to be drawn is that Tolkien has advanced Coleridge's claim for the true value of the imagination. For him the Secondary Imagination is to be seen as an "echo" of the Primary Imagination, which he had regarded as "the living power and prime Agent of all human perception and as a repetition of the finite mind of the eternal art of creation in the infinite I AM" (*Biographia Literaria,* Chap. XIII). The fairy story, the making of a Secondary World,[18] is a construct of the Imagination for Tolkien, just as the world is the creation of God the Creator. Thus all stories of "Faërie," and the trilogy is a notable example, look "forward or backward...to the Great Eucatastrophe" and partake of its epic and symbolic character. Since for Tolkien the Gospel story is true, by a transference of the transcending validity of the happy issue to the individual's battle with the World of Evil, he declares in *The Lord of the Rings* that "God is the Lord of angels, and of men — and of elves. Legend and History have met and fused" (p. 72).

The many legends referred to in the essay — the magic land of Hy Breasail in the West; Layamon's Story of King Lear in his *Brut;* the *Thrymskvitha* in the Elder Edda; the Shield-Kings of Denmark; the tale of Ingeld and his love for Freawaru; Sigurd of the Volsungs — are desperately serious for Tolkien, and so, he argues, should they be for us. They are, in a very literal sense, "requiring to be understood." Magic must be taken seriously in medieval story (e.g., *Sir Gawain and the Green Knight*), in eastern tale (e.g., the Egyptian *Tale of the Two Brothers*), or in modern fairy tale. And

Tolkien chides Sir George Dasent for forbidding children
to read two of his more "adult" tales, and quotes with
approval the anecdote of Chesterton's concerning children who were dissatisfied with Maeterlinck's *Blue Bird*
"because it did not end with a Day of Judgment" (p. 43).
  These thoughts indicate the moral and theological
concern which Tolkien posited for fairy story, and they
are underscored by his view that Elfland depends on
keeping promises and, ideally, on fulfillment of the
"oldest and deepest desire...the Escape from Death." It
is finally made clear that ideally "every writer making
a secondary world...every sub-creator, wishes in some
measure to be a real maker," to touch on "the serious
and dangerous matter...the Christian story" for it "has
long been my feeling (a joyous feeling) that God redeemed the corrupt-making creatures [by] the Great Eucatastrophe[,] The Christian joy." The religious and literary conclusion is that story or Art, the "Primary Art,
that is, of Creation," are all come together in "the
eucatastrophe of Man's history," "the Birth of Christ"
(pp. 70-72). Thus it is made clear that it was Tolkien's artistic purpose in his own subcreating to pro-
vide an analysis for his own generation, and those to
follow, of that point of fusion of all creation and of
its implications for the duty and destiny of humanity.
  Tolkien insisted that to be complete the fairy tale
or myth must have the eucatastrophe, since in its highest form myth dealt with the universal or cosmic reality, and that there must be progression, since myth is
meant to tell the whole story of its world from beginning to end. With the eucatastrophe comes joy and that
is really the beginning.[19] While the formal and earthly
historical process was brought to an end in Lewis's
Narnia, and it was the reality of the afterlife which
was beginning, the end for Tolkien's Middle-earth is
still remote in time and space. As Gandalf says, "There
are other men and other lives, and time still to be"
(III,87). Yet we are given to understand that the end
is there and that elves and Ring-bearers await it in the
undying lands. Already the process of history has removed whole civilizations[20] and even now, "much that was
fair and wonderful shall pass for ever out of Middle-
earth" (II,155). Lewis it was, writing on Macdonald,
who neatly summed up the attitude of his friend: "All

romantics are vividly aware of mutability, but most of them are content to bewail it: for Macdonald [and, we might add, for Tolkien] this nostalgia is merely the starting point — he goes on and discovers what it was made for."[21]

Although he does not discuss it in the expository essay, Tolkien is aware of the related problem of the apparent conflict between Destiny and Free Will, if the fruition of God's purposes is the true goal of Man. This issue, like that of the recurrence of evil (and the task of every generation to attempt to remove it to the realm of future possibility, rather than present actuality), is not discussed in Tolkien's critical work, but allowed to make its own impact in the writing itself.

Because of the refusal of critics to accept the trilogy on its own terms as myth, there has been considerable confusion about its genre and this doubtless explains the 1964 reissue of the fairy-story essay, as well as the Oxford-discussion sermons which Tolkien gave at various times, particularly at Pusey House in the decade following the publication of the trilogy. It may easily be shown that Tolkien's aim was not to produce a naturalistic novel so much as to restore the hero to modern fiction, and Christianity to a central position in men's thoughts. There is contained in the trilogy all the necessary material for religion. Conscience is presented in the form of an awareness of natural law, as the sense of fitness in the hobbits, and this in a form that is intuitive and emotional rather than rational. Lewis, elaborating on his friend's theory, was right to stress that "our victory is impermanent" and that the moral is "a recall from facile optimism and wailing pessimism alike to that hard, yet not quite desperate, insight into Man's unchanging predicament by which heroic ages have lived" (*T & C*, p. 15). In his review of the first volume, he most neatly summarized the position Tolkien posited for modern man: "There was sorrow then too, and gathering dark, but great valour, and great deeds that were not wholly vain. *Not wholly vain* — it is the cool middle point between illusion and disillusionment."[22]

In the year in which he revised the text of the Andrew Lang lecture as "On Fairy-Stories" (1947), Tolkien published a most subtle story which can be regarded

as an allegorical exemplum for the essay and may be
related to it, since both "were written in the same
period" as the early stages of *The Lord of the Rings*.
Although it can be understood as an illustration of the
writer's "wholly unsatisfied desire...[for] forests," it
is also related to his account of the student of fairy
stories "collecting only a few leaves, many of them now
torn or decayed, from the countless foliage of the Tree
of Tales, with which the Forest of Days is carpeted. It
seems vain to add to the litter. Who can design a new
leaf? The patterns from bud to unfolding, and the colours from spring to autumn were all discovered by men
long ago. But that is not true. The seed of the tree
can be replanted in almost any soil, even in one so
smoke-ridden (as Lang said) as that of England" (p. 56).
The passages also remind us of his 1927 chapter in *The
Year's Work in English Studies* in which he had referred
to *Germanica* as a "tree of altogether larger girth and
bigger branches."

But it is to the essay on fairy stories that we need
to refer for illumination of his attitude toward trees.
The awe and reverence he has for them is part of "the
wonder of things." It is clear that the hierarchy of
the imagination is to be found in the growing world.
While a leaf is a new story, an attempt to catch "Faërie"[23] in a net of words (although this is never quite
successful in this world, for the sought after is "in-
describable, though not imperceptible," p. 10), the tree
is the mass of tales which the mind can take in. The
forest is the continuous manifestation of time itself.
As Tolkien the theorist observed: "Each leaf, of oak and
ash and thorn, is a unique embodiment of the pattern,
and for some eye this very year may be *the* embodiment,
the first ever seen and recognized, though oaks have put
forth leaves for countless generations of men" (p. 56).

And yet these further dimensions of the little tale
are perhaps to be put aside for the moment, as Tolkien
lets it slowly unravel. The opening and certain of the
details inevitably suggest C. S. Lewis's *The Great Divorce* (1946), a kind of Harrowing of the Hell which man
makes of his own world. Some have seen the text as a
rebuttal of George Santayana's conception of immediate
joy, our direct pleasure in beautiful objects wherein
the human spirit is freed from "supernatural interfer-

ence." (See, for instance, *The Realm of Essence* [1927] and *The Realm of Matter* [1930], or the 1936 collection, *The Philosophy of Santayana*.)

The concept of the "journey" mentioned by Tolkien in the first sentence is not specific, and the notion of its being that of death itself is not made clear until the epilogue. Niggle, as he is first presented to us, is a man of no consequence, with an awkward journey ahead of him, a painter whose work is continually interrupted by "things he thought were a nuisance; but he did them fairly well, when he could not get out of them: which (in his opinion) was far too often." In a fashion, he was kind of heart, although he often ignored its promptings and would grumble and swear a little to himself. He assisted his neighbor, Parish, a man with a lame leg, and even others from further off, for "There were many things that he had not the face to say *no* to, whether he thought them duties or not; and there were some things he was compelled to do, whatever he thought" (p. 90). In short, Niggle was a quiet little Everyman, "a very ordinary and rather silly little man."

His painting is very important to him — perhaps the painting of the tree is symbolic of his life on earth — and he tries hard at it, although thoughts of the journey also slow down his work, as do the interruptions and the obligations to do things. He had started a number of paintings and not got far with them, since his skill was with leaves rather than trees, even though he did want to paint a whole tree. Finally, while he was working hard at "a leaf caught in the wind,...it became a tree." The process of artistic creation is well described in the way that this central trunk sends out more branches, fantastic roots, and acquires birds on its twigs, until finally a whole country opens out, with glimpses of a forest marching and the distant tips of mountains. It is possible to see the mountains in the background as glimpses of the spiritual lands of heart's desire, grasped by Niggle by virtue of his activities as a subcreator. Whatever else he has done is either discarded or incorporated into the new picture that soon takes up a whole shed, which stands where he had once grown potatoes. Despite a lack of encouragement — for he lives alone — Niggle feels that the picture is "wholly unsatisfactory and yet very lovely," and that if

it can stop growing, it will have to be finished. Yet
the more he tries to concentrate, the more interruptions
there are.

     At this point there is the intrusion of the town,
symbolic of man's obligations to his community. He is
wanted on a jury, and there are sent to him acquaint-
ances to take tea in his "pleasant little house, miles
away from the town." Although he resents the contact of
the town in the summer and when he is painting, he is
glad enough to go there to the shops and visit his ac-
quaintances in the winter. It serves as the greater
symbol of community, from which he may not cut himself
off, just as he may not completely ignore the continual
complaints about the weeds in his garden. The lesser
society of which he is a part consists of his lame
neighbor, Parish, and the latter's selfish wife, who is
ill, at a time when the wind has blown many tiles off
their roof, and the husband cannot cycle for a doctor or
the builders. Once he sets out on this errand, Niggle
is given a vision of the way to paint the "peak of a
snow-mountain," which had been tantalizing him, although
he doubts whether he will have the chance to effect
these strokes. The ride in the rain gives him a fever,
during which there are "marvellous patterns of leaves
and involved branches forming in his head and on the
ceiling"; and he buries himself in leaves, but after an
apparent recovery he is summoned to give up his canvas
to repair the roof of Parish's house, and then ordered
to start his journey immediately, although "it's a bad
way to start on your journey, leaving your jobs undone"
(p. 96).

     The best-known critic of both "Tree" and "Leaf" is
Colin Wilson in his essay, *Tree by Tolkien,* originally
published in late 1973, at about the time Tolkien
died.[24] Apart from stressing the influence of Chesterton (p. 12), Yeats (p. 14), and de la Mare (p. 16), he
draws attention to the Kafka-esque mode and details of
"Leaf":

> While [Niggle] is in bed, a strange Kafka-esque
> official calls on him and tells him that his neigh-
> bour's house is not satisfactory — the implication
> being that it is Niggle's duty to take care of his
> neighbour. Niggle's picture would be just the right
> size to mend a hole in Parish's roof. When Niggle

protests, "It's my Picture," the Inspector replies, "I dare say it is. But houses come first. That is the law." The bewildered artist is ordered to start on his journey, and he sets out quite unprepared. The journey is pure Kafka. (*Tree by Tolkien*, p. 23)

Niggle is soon on his way, although he manages to lose the few things he has with him when he gets out of the train, and so he is put in the Workhouse Infirmary. "This turns out to be a kind of prison where he is made to do boring manual tasks (it sounds like a Soviet labour camp) and spend hours locked in his room in the dark" (*Tree by Tolkien*, p. 23). While he endures these disciplines he reflects that he should have acted sooner for his neighbor, and then so many of the consequences of his selfishness need not have followed. Significantly he is employed at the very practical jobs he had not turned his hand to for his neighbor, but after a period of service he learns how to become master of his time, now without any sense of inner tension. His next treatment is digging, until he is on the point of collapse, after which, as he rests in the dark, he listens to the judges of the Court of Inquiry on himself. The weaknesses of his position are put by the First Voice: his heart did not function properly; he hardly ever thought at all and did not get ready for his journey; although he was moderately well off, he arrived almost destitute; he neglected the things ordered by the law;[25] he resented "interruptions" and uttered complaints and silly imprecations. The Second Voice, defending, notes that: his heart was in the right place; he was never meant to be anything very much, and he was never very strong; his painting, "a Leaf by Niggle," has a certain charm and "he took a great deal of pains with leaves, just for their own sake. But he never thought that that made him important; he did answer a good many calls, and never expected any return." His last act, the ride for assistance in the wet, is held to weight the scale, and make the case for a little gentle treatment, at which Niggle blushes: "that Voice...made Gentle Treatment sound like a load of rich gifts, and a summons to a King's feast" (p. 101). His basic decency is made clear by his first question, which is for Parish's welfare (p. 101).

Niggle awakes to sunlight, fresh clothing, and a light repast which is in the form of a communion, al-

though not so explicit. His new journey with a ticket
takes him to a Happy Land by train, bicycle, and path,
over the turf to a tree: "Before him stood the Tree, his
Tree, finished. If you could say that of a Tree that
was alive, its leaves opening, its branches growing and
bending in the wind" (p. 103). Here the sun is "very
bright," colors brilliant, the wind invigorating, everything seems new and smells are delicious. It is all
familiar as from a dream as "Niggle had so often felt or
guessed, and had so often failed to catch." It is perhaps this realization of his aspirations which really
suggests that Niggle is dead, for here the imagination
is truly liberated: "'It's a gift,' he said. He was referring to his art, and also to the result; but he was
using the word quite literally. He went on looking at
the Tree. All the leaves he had ever laboured at were
there, as he had imagined them rather than as he had
made them" (p. 104). What is most surprising is that
some of the most beautiful, characteristic, and perfect
leaves were seen to have been produced in collaboration
with Parish. Now, too, the further vistas are clearer
— birds, Forest, and the Mountains glimmering far away.
He has experienced a form of Recovery, in that he is,
for the first time, able to walk into the distance without turning it into mere surroundings. His artistic
temperament immediately discerns that there are "a number of inconclusive regions" that still need work, while
the Mountains are another picture, still to be per-
ceived.

On sitting to ponder how to approach his tasks,
which have a further quality which needs to be appre-
hended, "something·different, a further stage," he
thinks of Parish as flower lover and gardener, and the
latter appears, whereupon they both set to work without
any talk. Now their roles are reversed; each compen-
sates for his previously limited perspective. Niggle
is the better at ordering his time, while Parish often
wanders about looking at trees. Then, as in Naming Day
in Eden, Niggle, like Adam, imagines into existence
"wonderful new flowers and plants," while his friend
always knows exactly how to set them. Parish, who explains that he was able to come because Niggle had
wanted him, has now lost his limp, which was perhaps a
sign of spiritual malformation, and all tension between

them ceases after they have drunk from the "Spring in the heart of the Forest,...the source...and the nourishment of all that grew in the country."

In the spring of the year, with the Great Tree in full blossom, they walk to the margin of the country, the Edge (a phrase used also in *The Hobbit*), where they are met by a guide. While Parish, not yet ready to go on, waits there for his wife, Niggle passes on into Niggle's Country, a little bit of which is now Parish's Garden. Thus, the unimaginative and prosaic man has been blessed with imagination and become a subcreator himself. As the guide explains, it was all thought of by Niggle, although Parish and his wife had seen it only as Nonsense, or "That Daubing": "'But it did not look like this then, not *real*,' said Parish. 'No, it was only a glimpse then,' said the man; 'but you might have caught the glimpse, if you had ever thought it worth while to try'" (p. 109). To this Niggle immediately retorts that he had not given Parish much chance, mentally calling him "Old Earth-grubber": "'But what does it matter? We have lived and worked together now. Things might have been different, but they could not have been better.'" The acts of shared creation have brought mutual understanding and harmony.

Niggle turns to go further in, like the man who was saved in *The Great Divorce,* or the survivors of the Old Narnia, who were to reach the real country. In the process of further growth the little man is to learn of animals, higher lands, a wider sky, to go nearer the Mountains, and like Bunyan's Pilgrim to proceed "always uphill."

There follows an epilogue which is the earthly inquest on Niggle, at which the man of affairs states that he would have put him away, and thus have had him "start on the journey before his time," since he had indulged in private daydreams, and he did not live in the town, which is to be equated at last with practical or economic use of things. While dismissed by most, Niggle is remembered by the schoolmaster who, finding the corner of canvas with the one beautiful leaf, had preserved it in a museum, where it was finally burned in a fire, and then painting and man "were entirely forgotten in his old country." Yet the fact of Niggle's existence and his greatest creative achievement have meaning, for, as the two Heavenly Voices explain, that painted scene, an area of the human mind, has full reality in what we can now see is a transformed Limbo, which "is splendid for convalescence; and not only for that, for many it is the best introduction to the Mountains. It works wonders in some cases" (p. 112). The place has now been named, by the Porter, Niggle's Parish, a title which has caused both of them to laugh so that the Mountains rang.

This story is, more than anything else Tolkien wrote, an allegory of his own and the artist's creative exercise on earth, of its function in helping him and others on the spiritual journey. For the subcreation becomes a reality which one lives until he is ready to go on the spiritual journey towards the higher state represented by the Mountains.[26] The early part of the story, like the curious epilogue with its conversation between unimaginative "practical" men in civil authority on the subject of Niggle's life, presents the conflict between those who are of the spirit, represented on earth by imagination, and those who are not. The man of creative intellect is often bothered by what appear to be extraneous influences which retard his attempts to realize his vision. Colin Wilson writes: "The final judgement...is unexpectedly complex. In the conflict between the artist and society, Tolkien comes down on the artist's side — as is to be expected — but he also blames the artist, implying that if he were less vague and incompetent, he could become something more like a leader of society — without, however, compromising his own basic vision."[27]

In the terms of the story, even as the (potential) artist has responsibilities toward his fellows, so the more practical man of affairs needs to have sympathy toward his imaginative brother, without whose help he will never leave the Workhouse,[28] let alone see the Forest, or be introduced to the Mountains.

The story is also important in showing that Tolkien at this time was actively engaged in putting his ideas into allegorical form. The critic is the safer in the assumption that he might have been doing the same in *The Lord of the Rings*, particularly in the challenge which the imagination poses to the plain everyday existence of the hobbits.

"Leaf by Niggle" is distinctive in that it draws on no associations of the Germanic or Celtic past, but rather has affinities, if these can be discerned, with the medieval drama *Everyman,* with Bunyan, or with the more specifically allegorical journeys in the writings of C. S. Lewis. Yet its concern is to stress that "the business of the artist is to create a kind of tree as given and alive as possible. The tree will serve its purpose in a world that becomes increasingly urbanised."[29]

The story, more than the essay, is an exploration of the difference between the states of life lived prosaically, life with imagination, and life after death, for, by an intensification of some aspects of earthly life, the individual is translated to a different plane. While for "Leaf" "one of its sources was a great-limbed poplar tree that...was suddenly lopped and mutilated by its owner," this has surely been transmuted into the "Tree of Tales" which every man of vision can glimpse, even if it is not in his earthly powers to give actuality to the leaf which is the testimony to the value of the seed planted in the most arid soil, the soul of "a very ordinary little man."

Notes

1. W. H. Auden, for example, as critic of Tolkien usually chose to stress the quest, the heroic journey, the Numinous Object, and the victory of Good over Evil, as in his "At the End of the Quest, Victory," *New York Times Book Review,* January 22, 1956, p. 5, and in "The Quest Hero," *T & C,* p. 40, but he built his own criticism on Tolkien's essay in his *Secondary Worlds,* T. S. Eliot Memorial Lectures (London, 1968), particularly pp. 49-53.
2. Introductory note to *Tree and Leaf,* in *Tolkien Reader,* p. 2.
3. *Beowulf* essay, pp. 63f.   4. While these matters occur in various scholarly and creative pieces, the most interesting probing occurs in his "English and Welsh," being pp. 1-41 of *Angles and Britons* (Cardiff, 1963), a collection of O'Donnell Lectures by various hands.   5. "Philology: General Works," *The Year's Work in English Studies* (hereafter, *YWES*), 5 (1924), 65.
   6. *YWES,* 6 (1925), 32.   7. Lewis, "The Gods Return to Earth," *Time and Tide,* 14 Aug. 1954, pp. 1082-83; and "The Dethronement of Power," *Time and Tide,* 22 Oct. 1955, reprinted in

T & C, pp. 12-16.   8. Chesterton, *Orthodoxy* (London, 1908), pp. 66-102.   9. Macdonald, *Orts* (London, 1882), pp. 1-45. 10. The "cook" as artist, or even as an image of God as Creator, is the point of *Smith of Wooton Major* (1967). 11. Barfield, another of the circle of friends and writers, is an anthroposophist who holds that the solid objects of the material world are but the antecedent condition for perceiving the "unrepresented" noumenal world, so that man, in failing to acknowledge this Reality, has forgotten that all his knowing is ultimately a participation in the creative Word of God. 12. See Dawson, *Progress and Religion* (London, 1929), pp. 86ff. 13. Tolkien, "Chaucer as a Philologist," *Transactions of the Philological Society, 1934,* pp. 1-70.   14. Willoughby, *Transactions of the Philological Society, 1935,* p. 75.   15. Lewis, *T & C,* pp. 15f. 16. Many critics have found elements of Kafka in various parts of Tolkien's writing. See later pages in this essay for Colin Wilson's response to "Leaf by Niggle."   17. The subtitle of *The Hobbit* is *There and Back Again,* a term from Hegel which recurs in Tolkien's work and indicates the final value of distant *aventures* in the Blakean fight which then enable the hero to fight at home.   18. As W. H. Auden, Tolkien's disciple, put it in *Secondary Worlds,* "Present in every human being are two desires, a desire to know the truth about the primary world, the given world outside ourselves...and the desire to make new secondary worlds of our own, or, if we cannot make them ourselves to share in the secondary worlds of those who can" (p. 49).   19. This is similar to the end of *The Last Battle* (1956), the Narnia story by C. S. Lewis.   20. It is stressed in the trilogy that death is the *gift* of the One to men. 21. Lewis, in *George Macdonald: An Anthology* (London, 1946), p. 19.   22. Lewis, in *Time and Tide,* 14 Aug. 1954, p. 1083.   23. When Frodo can but recall parts of his elegy on Gandalf, these are described as "only snatches...faded as a handful of withered leaves" (I,374).   24. The actual limited English edition which came first in 1973, is not followed, but rather the more readily available American edition of 1974, published by Capra in their Chapbook Series.   25. Stern as this sounds, it probably refers to no more than the customary (Christian) courtesy to others which is innate in the hobbits and practiced almost automatically. 26. Presumably this quality of higher growth is similar to the function of the Sea and the Far West in *The Lord of the Rings.*   27. Wilson, *Tree by Tolkien,* p. 25.   28. Many of these images recall those of the Prison in *Pilgrim's Regress* (1933) by C. S. Lewis, a work which was subtitled *An Allegorical Apology for Christianity, Reason, and Romanticism.* 29. Wilson, p. 39.

....

Verlyn Flieger

FRODO AND ARAGORN: THE CONCEPT OF THE HERO

....

J. R. R. Tolkien once said that his typical response to
the reading of a medieval work was the desire not so
much to make a critical or philological study of it as
to write a modern work in the same tradition.[1] In *The
Lord of the Rings* he has done exactly that. The book is
a modern work, but in style and content it is certainly
in the medieval tradition. I do not propose to assign
The Lord of the Rings to a particular genre, such as
fairy tale, epic, or romance. The book quite clearly
derives from all three, and to see it as belonging only
to one category is to miss the essential elements it
shares with the others. More to the point is the way in
which Tolkien has used these elements.

What precisely is the appeal of a modern work in a
medieval tradition? What is the value of such a book
to the common reader? Why not offer him a bona fide
medieval work, *Beowulf* or *Sir Gawain and the Green
Knight,* and leave the twentieth century to the modern
novel? An answer may be found in Tolkien's essay "On
Fairy-Stories." Borrowing a term from G. W. Dasent,
Tolkien speaks in this essay of the "soup" of story,[2]
that rich mixture which has been simmering since man
first told tales, from which stories have been ladled
out to nourish the imagination in every age, including
our own. Although the soup is a blend of many morsels,
certain elements, certain flavors, stand out and evoke
immediate response. These are the basics, the raw stuff
of myth out of which folktale, fairy tale, epic, and
romance are fashioned. They are the motifs which recur
in all mythologies and which tale-tellers have used time

out of mind — the hero, the quest, the struggle with
monstrous forces of evil, the ordeal and its outcome.
They recur because they work, because they move the
reader and put him in touch with what is timeless. A
modern use of these motifs reaffirms their value as a
vital part of literature in an age when only scholars
and children (and too few of those) read the story of
King Arthur, or of Jack the Giant-Killer, or the adventures of Sigurd dragon-slayer.

The conventional medieval story, whether epic, romance, fairy tale, or some combination of these, most
often focuses on one figure — the hero of the tale. If
it is romance or epic the hero will be of great stature,
a larger-than-life Beowulf, or Galahad, or Arthur, or
Sigurd. If it is a fairy tale he may be a common man
like ourselves, the unlikely hero who stumbles into
heroic adventure and does the best he can — Jack, who
trades a cow for beans, or the miller's youngest son who
inherits only Puss-in-Boots. Larger-than-life heroes
are rare in twentieth-century literature; they do not
fit comfortably in an age which seems preoccupied with
the ordinary. But the little man is always with us, as
alive in the films of Chaplin as he is in Chaucer.

In *The Lord of the Rings* Tolkien has written a medieval story and given it both kinds of hero, the extraordinary man to give the epic sweep of great events, and
the common man who has the immediate, poignant appeal of
someone with whom the reader can identify.

Aragorn is a traditional epic/romance hero, larger
than life, a leader, fighter, lover, healer. He is an
extraordinary hero who combines Northrop Frye's romance
and high mimetic modes. He is above the common herd.
We expect him to be equal to any situation. We are not
like him, and we know it. We admire him, but we do not
identify with him.

Frodo, on the other hand, is a fairy-tale hero. He
is a little man both literally and figuratively, and we
recognize ourselves in him. He is utterly ordinary, and
this is his great value. He has the characteristics
also of Frye's low mimetic hero, the hero of realistic
fiction. He has doubts, feels fear, falters, makes mistakes; he experiences, in short, the same emotions we
experience. He is a low mimetic hero thrown by circumstances not of his making into high mimetic action. The

ways in which he deals with that action — coping with
burdens that are too great, events that move too swift-
ly, trials that are too terrible — draw the reader into
the narrative, so that he lives it with Frodo as he
never could with Aragorn.

A look at the two side by side shows that each
throws the other into greater relief, providing contrast, and enriching and expanding the dimensions of the
story. Having provided his book with an essentially
epic hero and an essentially fairy-tale hero, Tolkien
combines, and sometimes crosses, the characteristic motifs of each. Each hero has an extraordinary beginning.
Each undertakes a dangerous quest and undergoes ordeals.
But the parallels serve to heighten the contrast between the two. Aragorn's is a true quest to win a kingdom and a princess. Frodo's is rather an anti-quest.
He goes not to win something but to throw something
away, and in the process to lose all that he holds dear.
In simplest terms Aragorn's is a journey from darkness
into light, while Frodo's is a journey from light into
darkness — and out again. Aragorn derives from the pattern of the youthful hero, while Frodo has the characteristics of the hero come to the end of his adventures.
Tolkien gives Aragorn the fairy-tale happy ending — the
princess and the kingdom. To Frodo come defeat and disillusionment — the stark, bitter ending typical of the
Iliad, Beowulf, the *Morte d'Arthur.*

This crossing of motifs is not uniform, since Tolkien allows each hero enough of his typical characteristics to be recognizable. The motifs do cross, however,
at crucial points in the narrative, and at psychologi-
cally important moments in the unfolding of each character. I hope to show that this crossing of motifs adds
an appeal which few modern readers find in conventional
medieval literature, and that by exalting and refining
the figure of the common man, Tolkien succeeds in giving
new values to a medieval story.

Let us begin, however, with Aragorn, the larger-
than-life hero. William Ready calls him "almost too
good to be human," implying that his goodness somehow
impairs his believability.[3] The fact is that many readers lack the background to recognize an Aragorn. Strider — silent, watchful, road-weary — is an attractive
figure. His steely presence, his air of being someone

dangerous to cross, his resourcefulness in crisis,
evoke a character out of the mythic American West — the
stranger in town — cool, alert, alone. He has that
quiet toughness we associate with our folk-heroes. But
in the transition from Strider to Aragorn much of that
folk-hero quality is lost, and with it his hold on our
imagination. Paradoxically, the more we know him the
less familiar he becomes.

He is in truth the traditional disguised hero, the
rightful king, in medieval romance terms the "fair unknown" who steps from the shadows into the limelight
when his moment comes. He is in the tradition of the
young Beowulf, the young Galahad, the boy Arthur, all
the heroes whose early years are spent in obscurity but
who are destined for greatness and whose birth or origin
foreshadows that destiny.

A few examples will clarify the point. The medieval
account of the hero frequently includes his *compert,* or
conception. The conception episode almost always involves some element of magic or the supernatural. Prec-
edent for this comes from classical myth, where the hero
usually has one human and one divine or semidivine par-
ent. Achilles, Heracles, Theseus, and even so demon-
strably real a figure as Alexander the Great have divine
heritage.

The best-known story of the hero's *compert* is undoubtedly that of Arthur in Malory's retelling of the
Arthurian legend, wherein Merlin by his magic gives King
Uther access to Igraine's bed. From this meeting Arthur
is conceived. Thus the supernatural plays a part in Arthur's conception, even though both his parents are mortal. The conception of Galahad, later in the same book,
is a parallel. The sorceress Brusen contrives to en-
chant Lancelot and bring him to the bed of King Pelles's
daughter Elaine in the belief that she is Guenevere.
Here again immortal ancestry is replaced by the use of
magic in the conception of the hero. We find the same
convention in Celtic and Scandinavian myth. The Irish
hero Cuchulainn was fathered on a mortal woman by the
god Lugh. The Norse heroes Sigmund and Sigurd were descended from the god Odin. And on a more mundane level
the genealogies of kings in the Anglo-Saxon Chronicle
begin with Woden, the Germanic counterpart of Odin.

We will look in vain for any similar episode in Tol-

kien's account of Aragorn. No god's intervention, no
magic, enchantment, or supernatural events are to be
found. But Aragorn has immortal ancestry. It is not
immediate, as in the medieval narratives, but must be
traced back through many generations to an early union
of elves and men. In appendix A at the end of the trilogy, titled "Annals of Kings and Rulers," Tolkien makes
the following statement: "There were three unions of the
Eldar [elves] and the Edain [men]: Lúthien and Beren;
Idril and Tuor; Aragorn and Arwen. By the last the
long-sundered branches of the Half-elven were reunited
and their line restored" (III,314). It is clear that
Aragorn and Arwen each represents a branch of the half-
elven. They are descended from two brothers Elrond and
Elros, grandsons of the aforementioned Idril, an elf,
and Tuor, a man. Elrond, the father of Arwen, elected
to remain with the elves. Elros chose to go with men,
and became the first king of Númenor. His descendants,
through many generations, were Elendil and Isildur,
whose descendant and heir is Aragorn. In Tolkien's cosmology Aragorn's half-elven ancestry supplies him with
the immortal or supernatural origin necessary to the
hero figure.

The fact that Aragorn's immortal ancestry is played
down — indeed one has to look for it in order to find it
— is consonant with Tolkien's practice throughout the
book of providing realistic bases for what in a true medieval narrative would be frankly supernatural, marvelous, or miraculous. His goal is the one he outlines in
his essay "On Fairy-Stories," that is, "the realization
...of imagined wonder."[4] By "realization" he means just
what the word implies, *making real*. To make the wonderful as real as possible to his twentieth-century reader,
Tolkien surrounds it with the ordinary. We meet Strider; he is gradually revealed as Aragorn, and his immortal ancestry is buried in supplemental records and appendixes. Only after we believe him as a character are
we allowed to make the heroic associations that enrich
him and rank him with his predecessors in myth, epic,
and romance.

Another element, almost a necessity in the medieval hero pattern, is obscurity until the right moment.
Shadow provides contrast to light. Time after time we
read in medieval stories of the hero whose origins are

hidden, sometimes even from himself. He is buried in obscurity until the moment comes for him to step forward and announce himself by word or deed.

.   Often the obscurity of the hero is linked with his upbringing in a home not his own, in circumstances that train him for his future role but offer no recognition. Arthur is removed from his mother at birth by Merlin and brought up in the household of Sir Ector, ignorant, like everyone around him, of his royal lineage. The withdrawal of the sword from the anvil signals his emergence from obscurity and proclaims him as the rightful king.

Galahad, likewise, is raised in obscurity. Not until it is time for him to begin the Grail Quest is he introduced to Arthur's court. The event that announces his emergence as a hero is his withdrawal of the sword from the stone floating in the river below Camelot.

Germanic literature follows the same pattern. Sinfjotli, child of the incestuous union of Sigmund the Volsung and his sister Signy, is brought up by Sigmund in a secret woodland hideout until he is ready to avenge the slaying of his Volsung kin. Sinfjotli is fostered out to his own father, although both are ignorant of the relationship.

A hero who fits the pattern rather more loosely is Beowulf. He is not precisely raised in obscurity, but he is brought up in a home not his own, the court of his uncle Hygelac. We meet him first as a hero, and only after his killing of Grendel and Grendel's dam and his return in triumph to Hygelac's court do we learn of his unpromising beginnings.

> Long was he lowly,
> so that the sons of the Geats   accounted him not
>   excellent
> nor wished the lord of the Wederas   to give him
>   title to much
> on the mead-bench.   They deemed him slothful,
> high-born but unbold.[5]

In accordance with the established pattern, Aragorn comes from obscurity to recognition. Strider the Ranger is looked on with suspicion by even so good-hearted a man as Butterbur, the innkeeper at Bree. His true identity is concealed from all but a few until the time comes for him to reveal himself. Humphrey Carpenter has pointed out that in the first draft of the scene in the common room of the Prancing Pony the mysterious stranger was not a man, but a "queer-looking brown-faced hobbit," and his name was Trotter.[6] I suggest that such a character could not develop into the kind of figure that Strider was eventually to become. A disguised hobbit-prince would not fit into Tolkien's world and would be utterly out of place among the middle-class Boffins, Bolgers, Tooks, Proudfoots, and even the Sackville-Bagginses. The change from hobbit to man materially alters the possibilities for the character. The change of name, too, seems to signal the development of a more serious tone to the story. "Trotter" is simply not a name that can be taken seriously. The animal associations are too strong; it smacks too much of beast fable. One thinks at best of horses, and at worst of pigs. Carpenter remarks that in writing the preliminary chapters, "Tolkien was bending his tale away from the jolly style of *The Hobbit* towards something darker and grander, and closer in concept to *The Silmarillion*."[7] The alteration of the mysterious figure in the common room is certainly part of this change.

When he himself wrote of this first period of composition Tolkien said, apropos of the scene at Bree, "I had then no more notion than [the hobbits] had of what had become of Gandalf, or who Strider was; and I had begun to despair of ever finding out."[8] This provocative statement invites comment. Paul Kocher suggests that we can find in it part of the reason why Aragorn is difficult for readers. He simply has not been prepared for. Daniel Hughes goes further and suggests that it is just here, when Tolkien discovers who Strider is and what can be done with him, that the story begins to develop its epic side.[9]

If we take Tolkien's statement at face value we find him describing a situation not unfamiliar to writers: his narrative somehow got ahead of him. That unconscious process which often accompanies the conscious activity of the creative mind unexpectedly introduced new material. To be sure, this attitude suggests the traditional convention of authorial modesty: "I didn't write it; it wrote itself." But knowing as we do Tolkien's background in medieval literature it seems reasonable to suppose that he did have a stockpile of

literary raw material waiting to be used. We can perhaps credit his statement with a little less coyness and
a little more honesty than is usual in such cases.

What seems to have happened in the creative process
to translate Trotter into Strider and Strider into Aragorn is that Tolkien realized he had ready to his hand
in this mysterious figure the makings of an authentic
mythic hero, a medieval disguised prince. In the historical framework of Middle-earth, Aragorn is the lineal
descendant of Elendil, founder of the kingdoms of Arnor
and Gondor, and of Elendil's son Isildur, who took the
Ring from Sauron after defeating him in the Second Age.
Aragorn is therefore not only the rightful king of Gondor, but the rightful owner of the Ring. True to epic
convention, and also true to the circumstances of the
world that Tolkien creates, his identity is concealed,
with good reason. He is the son of Arathorn, a chief-
tain of the northern line of his house, killed when
Aragorn is a child of two. Aragorn is then taken by his
mother to Rivendell, where he is brought up in the house
of Elrond with Elrond's two sons. Aragorn is twenty
years old before Elrond tells him his true identity and
gives him the broken pieces of Elendil's sword, Narsil,
to keep until they can be reforged.

The giving and receiving of the sword calls up another medieval motif — the hero and his weapon. They
are inextricably linked, for the association of sword
and hero is more than a medieval convention: it is a
necessity in a literature which exalts heroism and deeds
of arms. Beowulf may slay Grendel with his bare hands,
but it takes a sword to kill Grendel's mother, a sword,
moreover, of no ordinary kind — "ealdsweord eotenisc" —
an ancient sword, made by giants.

Medieval literature is filled with swords as famous
and formidable as those who wield them. Many who know
no more of Arthur know of his sword Excalibur, and those
of other heroes are just as worthy of note. Beowulf's
sword, Næglfar, breaks in his death struggle with the
dragon. The dying Roland tries to break his sword Dur-
endal, so that none other shall ever use it. We have
seen that for both Arthur and Galahad the withdrawing
of a sword heralds the emergence of a hero.

The same motif occurs elsewhere. In the Norse
Volsungasaga Sigmund the Volsung pulls from a tree the

sword thrust into it by Odin, after others have tried
and failed. He carries it for the rest of his life. It
plays a curious role at the end of his adventures, when
it is broken, apparently deliberately, by Odin in Sigmund's last battle. After the breaking of the sword the
battle goes against Sigmund and he is killed. The fates
of sword and man are linked, and the destruction of one
signals the end of the other. The fragments of Sigmund's sword are saved for his son Sigurd and reforged
for the slaying of the dragon Fafnir. The reforging
of the sword and the slaying of the dragon with it mark
Sigurd's beginning as a hero.

Tolkien reworks this motif in fitting it to Aragorn.
At the Council of Elrond, where the decision is made to
take the Ring to Mordor, Aragorn stands before those
assembled and makes his declaration:

> He cast his sword upon the table that stood before
> Elrond, and the blade was in two pieces. "Here is
> the Sword that was Broken!" he said.
>
> "And who are you, and what have you to do with
> Minas Tirith?" asked Boromir, looking in wonder at
> the lean face of the Ranger and his weather-stained
> cloak.
>
> "He is Aragorn son of Arathorn," said Elrond,
> "and he is descended through many fathers from
> Isildur Elendil's son of Minas Ithil. He is the
> Chief of the Dúnedain in the North, and few are now
> left of that folk." (I,259f.)

With the casting of the sword upon the table Aragorn
publicly puts off Strider, assuming his rightful identity and all it implies. The sword proclaims the emergence of the hero. Arthur, Galahad, Sigmund, Sigurd,
all stand behind Aragorn in that moment. Tolkien is
careful, however, to keep Aragorn separate from them, so
that memories of the earlier heroes do not overpower his
narrative. Avoiding, then, the too-familiar motif of
the pulling out of the sword, Tolkien uses instead the
broken sword that is to be reforged. Defined strictly,
Aragorn is closer to Arthur or Sigmund than to Sigurd,
since he is a king, not a dragon-slayer. The unexpected
combination of king-hero with dragon-slayer's sword motif allows Aragorn to stand as a hero in his own right,
in his own narrative. We remember other heroes and
other swords, but we add a new figure to the line.

What gives Aragorn his most clear-cut romance characteristics is the part of the story that treats his
love for Arwen. The tradition of romantic love, which
requires the knight to endure hardships and perform
great deeds for the love of a lady, is necessary to the
characterization of Aragorn, for all that it is subordinate to the epic side of the narrative and remains
very much in the background.

As with his treatment of Aragorn's lineage, Tolkien
buries much of the material relating to Aragorn and Arwen in his appendixes, where the reader, if he looks,
will find the "Tale of Aragorn and Arwen." A few scattered references in the story proper relate them as romantic lovers; most of them do not even mention Arwen
by name. The clearest is, perhaps, a sly remark by
Bilbo at Rivendell, noting Aragorn's absence from the
feast, since "the Lady Arwen was there" (I,245).

The romance element is secondary to the epic struggle — the sweep of battle and great deeds. We know that
Aragorn is grimly engaged in winning his kingdom, but we
know almost nothing of his love for the half-elven princess for whom he wins it, nor do we realize until it is
all over that in winning the kingdom he is also winning
Arwen, and that one was a condition for the other.
Nonetheless a full understanding of Aragorn as a medieval hero must encompass knowledge of his love story, as
well as of his epic characteristics. Aragorn's is not
simply a political or national or even a personal epic
trial. It is also a trial of love, and in the light of
the love story, which we come to know only at the end,
the struggle and the battles take on a more specific and
personal meaning. The love story, too, is the perfect
vehicle for the fairy-tale happy ending, almost Eliza-
bethan in its rounding off of the story with celebra-
tions and marriages, of which Aragorn's and Arwen's is
the chief.

The romance element is manifest, too, in Aragorn's
capacity to heal and to renew. It has been plain from
the beginning of the story that Aragorn is a healer, for
his skill and knowledge of herb-lore pull Frodo through
in the first hours after he is wounded at Weathertop.
But at that point Aragorn is still Strider to the reader, and his ability to heal could well appear as practical knowledge of the road gained as a Ranger. Only much
later, when he has healed Éowyn and Faramir and Merry,

when the old wife Ioreth has told everyone who will listen that "*the hands of the king are the hands of a healer*" (III,136), does the reader recognize that Aragorn as healer and as king is what he has always been.

The concept of the king as healer derives from the early Celtic principle of sacral kingship, whereby the health and fertility of the land are dependent on the coming of the rightful king. Where there is no king, or where the king is infirm, the land also will be barren. This idea is most explicit in the Grail legend, with its association of the Waste Land with the Maimed King whose wound, sometimes specifically located in the thighs, is a wounding of virility extending from him to his kingdom. The Maimed King in the Grail stories is counterposed to the Healing King, the Grail Knight. In Malory's Arthurian story this is Galahad, whose healing of the Maimed King restores the land to fruitfulness. Tolkien makes full use of both these figures as the wasted lands of Middle-earth are restored to fruitfulness. Aragorn's is the positive role of healer and renewer, whose presence works to restore the land. Frodo, as I will subsequently show, becomes a kind of Maimed King figure, without whose sacrifice the efforts of the Healing King would be in vain.

All of the positive, glad-hearted, youthful elements of myth, epic, and romance cluster around the man we meet as Strider, whom we come to know as Aragorn. He is the recognized, acclaimed victor in the battle against evil, the king coming into his kingdom. He is warrior, lover, healer, renewer, a hero worthy of the heroic aspects of *The Lord of the Rings,* whose presence in the story at once contributes to and justifies those aspects.

Frodo is quite another thing. He is no Aragorn, no obscure hero awaiting his chance to be great. He is no warrior. And far from feeling destined for greatness, he reacts to being thrust into epic events with the cry of the common man — "Why me?" He knows, or thinks he knows, his own limitations and tells Gandalf, "I am not made for perilous quests" (I,70). He accepts an intolerable burden not from any sense that he is the proper one to bear it, but simply because no one else volunteers. It is worth noting, by the way, that another "little man" — Bilbo — does volunteer, and is gently

refused. The heroic figures all hang back, and the common man shoulders the burden. The point is voiced in
the narrative by Elrond, who says: "Yet such is oft the
course of deeds that move the wheels of the world: small
hands do them because they must, while the eyes of the
great are elsewhere" (I,283). This is almost a paraphrase of something Tolkien himself once said, recorded
by Carpenter: "The hobbits represent the combination of
small imagination with great courage which (as Tolkien
had seen in the trenches during the First World War)
often led to survival against all chances. 'I've always been impressed,' he once said, 'that we are here,
surviving, because of the indomitable courage of quite
small people against impossible odds.'"[10]
    Yet in spite of this surface appearance, Frodo like
Aragorn embodies mythic and heroic elements which supply
much of the strength of Tolkien's story. And there
stretches behind Frodo too a long line of mythic figures. He is linked unmistakably to the dying Arthur,
the dying Beowulf, the semimythical Scyld Scefing of the
opening lines of Beowulf, and the highly symbolic figure
of the Maimed King. Frodo becomes more than himself,
but it is Tolkien's great gift that in enlarging Frodo
he keeps him consistent with his beginnings. Frodo is
changed, but he is yet the same. That which is universal and symbolic is filtered through the particular and
literal. Frodo evokes the greater figures who stand behind him, but he is not engulfed by them. He remains
Frodo. In putting their burdens on his shoulders Tolkien has succeeded in synthesizing the medieval and the
modern, creating a character who conforms to mythic
patterns and yet evokes the identification and empathy
which the modern reader has come to expect from fiction.
    Frodo's beginnings are plain enough. He is the only
son of a middle-class hobbit couple, in no way unusual
except for the manner of their death — drowning in a
boating accident. But this is important, since Tolkien
emphasizes the fact that hobbits are as a rule shy of
boats and the water. They are inland people, hole-
builders, earth-dwellers. "Most Hobbits regarded even
rivers and small boats with deep misgivings, and not
many of them could swim" (I,16). The drowning of Frodo's parents is the key to one of his mythic functions,
for it is thematically important that Frodo should be

orphaned, and that his coming to Hobbiton be somehow
associated with water.

An outstanding figure in the mythologies of the
world is the child of mysterious or unknown origin who
arrives, sometimes in a boat, but always associated in
some way with water, and who brings with him extraordinary benefits. Perhaps the figure of this type most
familiar to the Western reader is the child Moses. But
to connect the mysterious child figure with Tolkien's
story we need go back no further than northern European
myth and literature.

The opening lines of *Beowulf* tell of Scyld Scefing,
the eponymous founder of the Scyldings, Hrothgar's line,
who led his people to victory in battle and brought them
unparalleled prosperity. He arrived as an unknown child
from the sea, and the poem describes the elaborate ship
burial that sends him back over the water. Scyld is
one avatar of a fertility figure ubiquitous in northern
mythology who appears under various names — Scyld,
Sceaf, Ing, Freyr, Frodi. They all have the same value
as bringers of peace and fertility, and they are more
or less connected — some remotely, some, like Scyld,
specifically — with water, with death, and with ships
and funeral ceremonies.

Frodo's association with the mysterious or orphan
child motif is evident, and the linking of that motif
with Scyld and Frodi as fertility figures suggests that
Tolkien wished to invest Frodo with the mythic significance of a bringer of peace, prosperity, and fruitfulness. The name Frodo, a variant of Frodi, is surely no
accident, no random choice to fit a furry-footed hobbit,
but one consciously chosen to state a connection Tolkien
wished to make. Carpenter's biography of Tolkien reveals that Frodo's name was originally Bingo, but Tolkien, as he wrote, grew more and more dissatisfied with
that name, and with good reason. Aside from its more
frivolous associations, it is phonetically too close to
Bilbo. The name remained Bingo, however, until Tolkien
found his story turning increasingly away from *The Hobbit* and in the direction of the older and darker subject
matter of *The Silmarillion*. At that point he changed
his hero's name to Frodo.

Frodo, the orphan associated with water, brings
peace, prosperity, and fruitfulness to the Shire, though

he himself can no longer benefit from them. In the end
he is committed again to the water, and like Scyld, is
sent over the waves to an unknown bourne.

Frodo, like Aragorn, like Arthur, Galahad, Beowulf,
is brought up in a home not his own, Bilbo's home. And
here another medieval motif enters, for Frodo is Bilbo's
nephew. The relationship of uncle and nephew, specifically uncle and sister's son, is prominent in medieval
narrative from *Beowulf* to Malory. Jessie Weston calls
it "a relationship obviously required by tradition" and
cites uncle-nephew pairs in both early and late medieval epic and romance.[11] Her list includes Cuchulainn
and Conchobar, Diarmid and Finn, Tristan and Mark, Roland and Charlemagne, and Gawain and Arthur. To these
we might add Mordred and Arthur, Sinfjotli and Sigmund
(these last two are incestuous, being son and father
as well) and Beowulf and Hygelac. What all these pairs
have in common is that some action initiated by the
uncle is brought to its conclusion, whether for good or
ill, by the nephew. In any case, the relationship is a
well-established and well-recognized literary motif.
We may be sure that Tolkien is giving us important information when he makes Frodo Bilbo's nephew.

The information is given obliquely, however, for,
as with Aragorn, Tolkien avoids a one-to-one correlation
between Frodo and earlier medieval heroes. Rather he
awakens echoes of the earlier stories which will enrich
his own narrative without defining it too narrowly.
Thus he does not introduce Frodo into the story as a
nephew, but as a cousin, and he employs a comic figure
— the Gaffer — to explain the relationship. "Mr. Drogo
he married poor Miss Primula Brandybuck. She was our
Mr. Bilbo's first cousin on the mother's side (her mother being the youngest of the Old Took's daughter's) and
Mr. Drogo was his second cousin. So Mr. Frodo is his
[Bilbo's] first *and* second cousin, once removed either
way, as the saying is, if you follow me" (I,31). It is
noteworthy that Frodo's mother is closest to Bilbo, being his first cousin, while Drogo is his second cousin.
The female side is stressed, and the sister's son relationship is thus obliquely alluded to.

A more specific linking of Frodo with Bilbo is given
in the Prologue, where Frodo is plainly called Bilbo's
"favourite nephew" (I,20). What is clear, then, is that

Tolkien is adding something important to his story by so
carefully underlining the relationship. Action initiated earlier by Bilbo — the finding of the Ring — will
be completed by Frodo, who accepts the responsibility of
throwing it away. This is the thematic basis for Elrond's gentle rejection of Bilbo's offer to carry the
Ring to Mordor. The task has passed from uncle to nephew. Bilbo cannot complete the action. It is Frodo in
the role of nephew who must carry it to an end.

Early in the narrative Frodo joins forces with Strider, who is all that Frodo appears not to be — big,
tough, experienced, a fighter and a doer, where Frodo is
small, sheltered, and unaccustomed to adventure. Beneath this surface disparity, however, Tolkien links his
heroes by providing each with a variant of the same epic
motif. We have already noted Tolkien's restructuring of
the medieval sword-motif to enrich the figure of Aragorn
and give him epic associations. Similar epic associations are given to Frodo as well, but they are scaled
down to hobbit dimensions and pass all but unnoticed in
the narrative.

As the Fellowship prepares to leave Rivendell with
the Ring there is a homely farewell scene between Bilbo
and Frodo:

> On the morning of the last day Frodo was alone with
> Bilbo, and the old hobbit pulled out from under his
> bed a wooden box. He lifted the lid and fumbled in-
> side.
>
> "Here is your sword," he said. "But it was bro-
> ken, you know. I took it to keep it safe but I've
> forgotten to ask if the smiths could mend it. No
> time now. So I thought, perhaps, you would care to
> have this, don't you know?"
>
> He took from the box a small sword in an old
> shabby leather scabbard. Then he drew it, and its
> polished and well-tended blade glittered suddenly,
> cold and bright. "This is Sting," he said, and
> thrust it with little effort deep into a wooden
> beam. "Take it, if you like. I shan't want it
> again, I expect."
>
> Frodo accepted it gratefully. (I,290)

More important than the sword itself is the manner
of its giving. Bilbo thrusts it into a wooden beam, re-

peating in unobtrusive fashion Odin's thrusting of the
sword into the tree for Sigmund. Frodo "accepts" it.
Tolkien does not say how. But to take it he must pull
it out of the beam in a repetition of Sigmund's withdrawal of his sword from the tree, Arthur's taking of
the sword from the anvil, and Galahad's withdrawal of
his sword from the stone floating in the river.

A mythic pattern underlies the giving and receiving
of the sword, but it has been displaced and fragmented
in *The Lord of the Rings*. What in the *Volsungasaga* was
one sword, broken with Sigmund and reforged for Sigurd,
is here two swords, and the order of events is reversed.
Frodo's old sword is broken, and is replaced by Sting.
Sting is thrust into the beam by Bilbo and withdrawn by
Frodo. The tone here is anything but epic. Instead of
a supernatural event we have a quiet conversation between old friends. The speech is familiar and colloquial — "don't you know," "if you like," "I expect." The
sword is small, the scabbard shabby. Bilbo fumbles in
bringing it out. The gesture of thrusting it into the
wooden beam is almost thrown away. The whole character
of the scene is touching rather than heroic.

The surface structure of this scene makes it clear
that the torch has passed. Bilbo's part in the story of
the Ring is over; Ring and sword have been handed on to
his nephew, who must undertake the quest. The underlying mythic pattern — the sword and the method of its
transfer — aligns Frodo with his epic forebears, and
with Aragorn as well.

Tolkien brings his two heroes together almost, it
would seem, in order to have them part. Having established each clearly, and put them side by side, he then
sends them in opposite directions — Aragorn west, expanding the scope and epic action of the story, Frodo
east, intensifying our focus on the perilous nature of
his quest and its effect on him. The journey into Mordor is, of course, Frodo's final test, the ultimate ordeal through which he must pass to his eventual apoth-
eosis. For it is on the journey to Mordor and in the
final moments at the Cracks of Doom that the crucial
event in the medieval hero-story, the confrontation and
struggle with the monstrous foe, embodiment of all the
forces of darkness, takes place.

To see this clearly we must first look at the thesis

of Tolkien's landmark essay "*Beowulf*: the Monsters and
the Critics." It is undoubtedly his best-known scholarly work. It is one of the few and certainly one of
the first critical essays that value *Beowulf* as a poem
rather than as a historical, or philological, or socio-
cultural artifact. *Beowulf,* says Tolkien, is a poem
about a man fighting with monsters — a manlike monster,
Grendel, who preys on men and eats them, and a dragon
who guards a hoard of gold. As such, the poem reflects
the northern imagination, whose vision is of "man at war
with the hostile world, and his inevitable overthrow in
Time." The monsters are all the forces of darkness
against which men have always struggled, and by which
they are always defeated. The poet's phrase "heroes under heaven" or "mighty men upon earth" evokes for Tolkien "*eormengrund,* the great earth, ringed with *garsecg,*
the shoreless sea, beneath the sky's inaccessible roof;
whereon, as in a little circle of light about their
halls, men with courage as their stay went forward to
that battle with the hostile world and the offspring of
the dark which ends for all, even the kings and cham-
pions, in defeat."[12]
     Clearly, for Tolkien, the monster figure is at the
heart of the matter. And, important as it is, we would
expect to find that he had placed such a figure at the
heart of *The Lord of the Rings.* As a story in the medieval tradition it should depend for its force as much on
the monster as on the hero. And where is there a monster who confronts and battles with the hero? There are
monstrous beings, to be sure, but in no case do they directly do battle with either hero. Aragorn fights orcs,
but not in single combat, and only as part of a larger
battle. Sam fights Shelob; Gandalf fights the Balrog.
The greatest evil is Sauron, the Enemy, the Dark Lord
for whom all the forces of darkness work. But he is
never seen. Aragorn and Gandalf do contend with him,
but at a distance, and indirectly. Furthermore, while
he is all evil, he is not concrete enough to fit Tolkien's criteria for monsters. For him they must be
"mortal denizens of the material world, in it and of
it."[13]
     I suggest that Tolkien's central monster-figure
is so natural a part of the material world that he
goes largely unrecognized as such. He is Gollum, the

twisted, broken, outcast hobbit whose manlike shape and dragonlike greed combine both the *Beowulf* kinds of monster in one figure.

To see Gollum as a manlike monster we must first accept his relationship to humanity. Tolkien makes it plain that Gollum is some kind of hobbit, "akin," says Gandalf, "to the fathers of the fathers of the Stoors." He goes on: "Even Bilbo's story suggests their kinship. There was a great deal in the background of their minds and memories that was very similar. They understood one another remarkably well, very much better than a hobbit would understand, say, a Dwarf, or an Orc, or even an Elf. Think of the riddles they both knew, for one thing." And though warped and grotesque, Gollum is not yet entirely lost to humanity. "There was a little corner of his mind that was still his own, and light came through it, as through a chink in the dark; light out of the past. It was actually pleasant, I think, to hear a kindly voice again, bringing up memories of wind, and trees, and sun on the grass, and such forgotten things. But that, of course, would only make the evil part of him angrier in the end" (I,62-64).

There we have him, of hobbit kind, murderer, outcast, maddened by reminders of joys he cannot share. He is even cannibalistic, for we learn in *The Hobbit* that he eats goblins when he can't get fish, and would have eaten hobbit if he had defeated Bilbo in the riddle game. The parallel with Grendel, the man-eating monster of *Beowulf,* is unmistakable. Grendel is outcast, a wanderer in the waste, of the race of Cain, the first murderer, and he cannot bear the sound of the harp and the song of creation.

Gollum's dragon features are not so apparent. His most obvious characteristic is greed for a treasure. Dragons are traditionally associated with hoards of gold, whereas Gollum wants only the one Ring, but the difference is quantitative, not qualitative. The most famous dragon in northern literature, Fafnir, transformed himself from man to dragon so he could guard his gold, of which the crucial portion was a ring. So Gollum, once a hobbit, has been transformed by his desire for the Ring into a creeping thing. His name, Sméagol, is related to a number of Anglo-Saxon words meaning to creep, to crawl, words used to describe dragons. His

very word for the Ring, "precious," is an Anglo-Saxon
word glossed by Klaeber in his edition of *Beowulf* as
maðum. It is a word used in *Beowulf* for treasure, and
specifically to refer to the dragon's hoard.
    Gollum is a combination, then, of manlike and drag-
onlike monster. But a monster figure must be defined
not just by what he is, but by what he does. The function of the monster in medieval narrative is to oppose
the hero, to body forth tangibly the evil to be overcome, to be the force against which the hero's strength
and courage are tested.
    It is typical of what I call Tolkien's modern medi-
evalism that having given his story a monster in the
person of Gollum he chooses for the monster's opponent
not the epic hero Aragorn, but Frodo, the little man who
feels he is not a hero and does not want to be one.
    The battle between them is central to a reading of
The Lord of the Rings as a modern work in the medieval
tradition. For the battle is psychological, not physical, and the battleground is Frodo himself. To expli-
cate this we must look carefully at the special relationship of Frodo and Gollum. As early as 1957 Douglass
Parker called Gollum "Frodo's corrupted counterpart."
Rose Zimbardo called him Frodo's "dark counterpart."
George Thomson put the relationship in perspective: "It
is a well-known fact of the romance tradition that because the principal characters are simple types the complexities of human nature must be projected into the
external world. The disruptive forces of darkness and
inner conflict must be represented by persons or objects
outside the heroic characters." Thus, Gollum as Frodo's
"double in darkness is more than a potentiality of his
own nature. His double is truly his, an actual and developing darkness in his own character."[14]
    Fiction abounds in dualities of this kind. Dr.
Jekyll and Mr. Hyde, Victor Frankenstein and his monster, Poe's William Wilson and his double are all
examples of what psychology calls the "self" and the
"other," that is, the overt personality and its opposite, the light and dark sides of one's nature. Jung
calls this other side of mankind the "shadow" as contrasted with the overt and recognized "ego." Often this
duality is presented as two aspects of one nature, as
with David Lindsay's Maskull and Nightspore, or as E. M.

Forster suggests may be the case with Virginia Woolf's
life-loving Mrs. Dalloway and the young suicide Septimus
Smith.

Frodo and Gollum can fit the same pattern, Frodo as
the self, Gollum as the other. Frodo is the overt, recognized character. Gollum is his dark side, the embodiment of his growing, overpowering desire for the
Ring, the desire which at last becomes all-consuming and
sweeps away (if only for a moment) the Frodo who has en-
dured so much to destroy the Ring. Gollum represents
precisely that "disruptive force of darkness and inner
conflict" which Thomson says must be shown to the reader
outside the heroic character. Gollum is what Frodo must
fight within himself as the Ring increases its hold.

I do not mean to present Gollum as an allegorical
personification. He is not simply an abstract quality
or a projection of a state of mind. Any careful reader
of *The Lord of the Rings* knows that Tolkien detested
allegory, and to impose it on his book is to do violence
to his intention. Gollum is a fully realized character
in his own right, with a considerable part to play in
the story. But he can suggest these other things as
well.

Today's reader of a modern narrative, however medieval its spirit, may be reluctant to accept a truly medieval monster — a dragon or a fiend — but he is accus-
tomed to accepting internal conflict, man warring with
himself, for that is what much of modern fiction deals
with. Frodo monster-queller might not be credible. But
Frodo tortured by growing evil in his own nature, fighting his great battle not against darkness without but
against darkness within, is believable and compelling.
In fighting those dark elements within himself which
Gollum externalizes, Frodo fights the most insidious and
powerful monster of all — and loses. Tolkien's picture
of the battle, although not literal, is very much in the
spirit of the northern imagination he describes in the
Beowulf essay. It is that battle against "the offspring
of the dark which ends for all, even the kings and cham-
pions, in defeat."[15]

In the final moment, standing at the Cracks of Doom,
Frodo succumbs to the darkness within him. He puts the
Ring on his finger, claimed by it even as he claims it.
The end is inevitable. For man always loses to the mon-

ster at last. Frodo is defeated just as surely as Beowulf is.

It is characteristic of Tolkien, however, that he does not end on this note. Frodo loses, but in losing he wins a greater victory. The climax is designed to show that just as surely as Frodo's action is inevitable, so is Gollum's. Frodo will put on the Ring and Gollum will be driven to seize it. In so doing he saves Frodo and destroys the Ring. Frodo's dark side, externalized as Gollum, destroys the actual dark within him, and the maddened Gollum, exulting in possession, falls with the Ring into the fire. Evil destroys itself.

Although Frodo recovers from the battle, he can no longer be what he was. He is wounded by sword, sting, and tooth, and cannot find healing. He now evokes the Maimed King of the Grail legend. The loss of his finger, seen by some critics as symbolic castration, could legitimately be interpreted as a version of the archetypal fertility wound of the Maimed King. Frodo is maimed, his loss of the Ring makes possible the renewal of the land, and, as in many versions of the Grail story, he is associated with and finally committed to water. His departure from Middle-earth to be healed of his wounds unmistakably evokes yet another wounded figure, the wounded Arthur, and his departure by ship to be healed of his wounds. It rounds off the association of Frodo with the mysterious child, with Scyld Scefing, and with those fertility figures mentioned earlier, who bring prosperity and peace.

The fairy-tale hero, inconspicuous and unassuming, has been made to suffer the bitterness and loss of the medieval epic hero. Like Beowulf, like Arthur, he loses the last battle and pays a heavy price for his struggle. Such an end is dreadfully inappropriate. If he is not given half the kingdom and the princess's hand in marriage he ought at least to be able to live happily ever after. He should get some recognition, some recompense. It is not fair.

And that, of course, is just Tolkien's point. It is not meant to be fair. We are beyond the epic now, beyond romance and beyond the fairy-tale ending. In the real world things seldom turn out as we would like them to, and the little man is as subject to tragedy as the great one. For Beowulf to die, for Arthur to lose Cam-

elot, these are, in their way, great endings to great
lives. They come at the end of brave days and brave
deeds. Their stories end not happily but fittingly, and
that is as it should be. To take the epic ending and
give it to the fairy-tale hero is to reveal new values
in the old pattern. The sacrifice is all the greater
for being made by one so small.
But the story must have Aragorn to give it point.
Without the two heroes much of the impact would be lost.
Frodo is the passing of the old, Aragorn the emergence
of the new. Both happen at the same time, and each because of the other.
Tolkien read *Beowulf* as a poem of balance, the opposition of ends and beginnings. He says of it: "In
its simplest terms it is a contrasted description of
two moments in a great life, rising and setting; an
elaboration of the ancient and intensely moving contrast between youth and age, first achievement and final
death."[16] He has built these same values, this same
balance and opposition, into *The Lord of the Rings* in a
synchronous rather than sequential pattern. By giving
us both Aragorn and Frodo he has used the contrast between them to widen and deepen the meaning of his story.

Notes

1. Richard C. West, "The Interlace Structure of *The Lord of the
Rings*," in *A Tolkien Compass*, ed. Jared Lobdell (LaSalle, Ill.,
1975), p. 80.   2. "On Fairy-Stories," pp. 19ff.   3. Ready,
The Tolkien Relation: A Personal Inquiry (Chicago, 1968), p.
101.   4. "On Fairy-Stories," p. 14.   5. *Beowulf*, lines
2184-88, author's translation.
6. Carpenter, *Tolkien* (Boston, 1977), p. 188.   7. Ibid.,
p. 186.   8. *Tree and Leaf* (Boston, 1965), p. vii.   9. Paul
Kocher, *Master of Middle-earth: The Fiction of J. R. R. Tolkien*
(Boston, 1972), p. 131; Daniel Hughes, "Pieties and Giant Forms
in *The Lord of the Rings*," in *Shadows of Imagination: The Fantasies of C. S. Lewis, J. R. R. Tolkien, and Charles Williams*,
ed. Mark Hillegas (Carbondale, Ill., 1976), p. 91; see p. 82.
10. Carpenter, p. 176.
11. Jessie L. Weston, *From Ritual to Romance* (Garden City,
N.Y., 1957), p. 191.   12. *Beowulf* essay, p. 67.   13. Ibid.,
p. 69.   14. Douglass Parker, "Hwaet We Holbytla...," *Hudson
Review*, 9 (1956-1957), 605; Rose A. Zimbardo, "Moral Vision in

....

The Lord of the Rings," *T & C,* p. 105; George H. Thomson, "*The Lord of the Rings*: The Novel as Traditional Romance," *Wisconsin Studies in Contemporary Literature,* 8, No. 1 (Winter 1967), pp. 51-53.   15. *Beowulf* essay, p. 67.
    16. Ibid., p. 81.

Rose A. Zimbardo

THE MEDIEVAL-RENAISSANCE VISION OF 'THE LORD OF THE RINGS'

In the course of this paper I will be talking about a
vision of cosmic harmony — the great *discordia concors* —
that was celebrated in English literature until the mid-
seventeenth century, when men — even poets, who should
have known better — discarded that image, as Tolkien's
friend, C. S. Lewis, tells us, and, in the spirit of Saruman, set up their own reason as their god and launched
us into the dark ages from which we are still struggling
to emerge. It is for that reason that I cannot label
the imaginative vision that shapes *The Lord of the Rings*
as either "medieval" or "Renaissance"; Lewis was, to my
mind, quite right in arguing the falsity of such a distinction.

What has always interested me about *The Lord of the
Rings* is its title. So sensitive was Tolkien to language, so fully aware that to "name" a power is to give
it life and even to become subject to it, that he surely
did not name his trilogy for Sauron, the Dark Lord, and,
as surely, the rings of his title are not to be identi-
fied with the terrible Ring of his tale. Who then is
the Lord of the Rings whom the title and the tale celebrate, and what is the nature of the rings that he
holds?

As we all know, Tolkien was a scholar as well as a
teller of tales; the conception of artistic "imitation,"
or the way that tale imitates truth, that he held is
that which dominates the thought of the period he studied. His conception is quite different from most post-
eighteenth-century conceptions of artistic imitation,
which, by attempting to shape art to the dimensions of

what can be empirically known, diminish the function of
art, narrow the conception of the "nature" that art imitates to the confines of human experience, and confuse
"realism" with reality. For Tolkien's conception of artistic imitation we must go back to the Renaissance com-
monplaces that associate the creative artist with the
Creator, that make his arena "the Globe," and that consider a work of art a design that, as Sidney says in
An Apologie for Poesie, "shewes such formes as nature,
often erring, would shew"[1] if she could. This esthetic
conception originates in the thinking of the late medieval commentators. As Hugh of St. Victor puts it:
"This entire perceptible world is as a book written by
the finger of God, that is created by divine power, and
individual creatures are as figures within it, not invented by human will (arbitrio), but instituted by Divine authority (placito) to make manifest the invisible
things of God."[2]

Conversely, for the medieval-Renaissance artist, a
book is a design of figures moving in an interrelation
that "makes manifest the invisible things of God"; it
is an imitation of the world, and, like the world, it
manifests the nature of the Creator. The Lord of the
Rings that Tolkien's trilogy celebrates is God, the Creator; the rings that he holds are the concentric circles
of all created life that stretch from the well-balanced
individual soul of each creature to the farthest reaches
of the cosmos — to sound what the Renaissance called
"the music of the spheres." Because Tolkien attempted
to revive the medieval-Renaissance conception of artistic imitation, he could slough off as irrelevant the
criticisms of those reviewers who faulted him for not
having "realistic characters" and could be impatient
with others who labeled his work an "allegory," as
though, to his mind, this whole world and all of us in
it were not an "allegory" of sorts.

Two principles govern the visionary world of *The
Lord of the Rings:* the twin principles that the Renaissance called "permanence in mutability" (the idea that
we find in Spenser's *Cantos of Mutabilitie*) and *discordia concors,* the idea that the harmony of the whole
of creation depends upon the variety within, and the
balance among, each of its parts. The time scope of *The
Lord of the Rings* implies vast reaches beyond the "last
battle" to which the narrative confines itself. The age

of wizards, elves, dwarves, men, and hobbits that we see is unique in itself (and insofar as it *is* unique, it must pass); but it is also a recapitulation of ages that have been, as the songs of the elves remind us, and it is also a preparation for ages to come. The temporal order that *The Lord of the Rings* implies is in itself a ring — the ring of endless renewal.

Each age must pass, but in every age, if the inhabitants of the world set right the balance of a time that may seem in their eyes to be "out of joint," if they capture the past in poetry — as the elves do — and if they plant seeds for coming generations, they can insure a new birth and can thereby contribute in their turn of time to the cycle of endless renewal. Each creature, each generation, each species must pass, because each is subject to the law of mutability, but their passage insures the birth of new ages. All forms of life are subject to change, but in that change nothing is lost. Gandalf the Grey goes through death and reemerges as Gandalf the White. The idea is perhaps best expressed by Golding, the Renaissance translator, who tells us in the introductory epistle to his translation of Ovid's *Metamorphoses:*

> Of this same dark Philosophie of turned shapes, the
>   same
> Hath Ovid into one whole masse in this book brought
>   in frame.
> Foure kinds of things in this his work the Poet doth
>   conteyne.
> That nothing under heaven doth ay in stedfast state
>   remayne.
> And next that nothing perisheth; but that each sub-
>   stance takes
> Another shape than that it had...
> Then sheweth he the soule of man from dying to be
>   free. (Introd. Ep.7-19)[3]

The temptation that the "One Ring" (and its terrible significance is that it is the *"One"* Ring, or the Ring of Oneness) has for Galadriel is the temptation that is presented to the powerful in every generation from the necromancer of the middle ages to the cryogenist of our own — to make *my* time all time, to make *my*self or *my* people immortal by freezing the cycle of regeneration to my own needs.

Galadriel's wisdom is sufficient to the test; she knows that her people must in their time "go West" and pass into another dimension of being in order for the seeds they have planted and the songs they have made to pass into the hands of a new age of creatures and thereby, curiously, to enter "the artifice of eternity" — the greater time that poetry imitates. Because she loves her people, and all living things, she knows that the only alternative to passage through time is enslavement in it. As she tells Frodo, who offers her the Ring, if she were to use it she would cease to be Galadriel, the soul of Lothlórien, and would become the "Terrible Queen," another Sauron, however good her original intention might seem to her to be. Galadriel's greatness rests upon her ability to see herself and her people as one part in a greater harmony that embraces them. It is by denying herself for the good of the whole that she preserves the integrity of her particular note in the harmony.

The structure of *The Lord of the Rings* shapes that harmony, the *discordia concors* that the world is when, in rightful balance, it reflects the greater, cosmic harmony. Tolkien uses the metaphor as it appears in Renaissance poetry and thought, where, as John Hollander reminds us, it was "interpreted in the old Pythagorean way as intervals produced by stopping a monochord" rather than in our modern conception of "the ordering of simultaneously sounding musical tones, taken as a 'package.'"[4] The image of the rightly balanced world appeared in the emblem books as a "well-tuned lyre," the emblem of Concord. Each note is separate, each unique, and the differences among them, as well as the distances between them, are essential to the harmony that they produce. That is why we have in *The Lord of the Rings* so many different creatures. That is why we have creatures whose natures are antithetical — like dwarves who live beneath the ground and work in metals, and elves who live above the ground and work in song — and who would war with each other if they were not held in proper alignment by the greater harmony, the ring of *discordia concors,* that together they comprise.

The distances between them — from "high" wizards to "low" hobbits — is equally vital to Tolkien's musical

metaphor. Those sloppy readers who have accused him of
expressing "aristocratic," or even "fascistic" political
attitudes in his work are, once again, reading in the
spirit of nineteenth-century naturalism. After all it
is the hobbits, the lowly provincials whom the seemingly
wise Saruman and Sauron have been too self-absorbed to
notice and whom only the truly wise Gandalf never under-
estimates, who emerge as the heroes of the work. They
are heroes because each maintains his own, and respects
other, individual integrity, and because of their inclination to fellowship. In right balance, when the
unique integrity of each part is preserved and when each
part is in rightful alignment with all other parts, the
world is a well-tuned lyre. That balance can be broken,
however, and the lyre unstrung if any part within it refuses to recognize that it *is* a part within a greater
whole, if any creature forgets the "ring" of *caritas* and
falls victim to *cupiditas,* the desire to make himself
his only good. It is pity for Gollum that saved Bilbo
in the past; it is Frodo's pity for Gollum, his own dark
doppelgänger, that preserves Gollum for the final part
he has to play. In fighting the Gollum in himself and
subduing it, Frodo (i.e., Frodo/Gollum) is able at last
to drop the Ring of Oneness — of falsely defined individuation — into the Crack of Doom. But, like Sir Gawain, he must bear the scar of this dubious conquest
even after his quest has been completed.

The moral import of Frodo's quest is as old as the
story of Lucifer's fall, and as new as today. We are
each of us "Ring-bearers," for the smallest but most
important of the "rings" that the great Lord of rings
holds is each creature's idea of self. A creature may
succumb to the power of the "One Ring," the delusion of
false individuation — the dark desire that lurks within
each of us to make all time and all other creatures subject to our own wills. In that case his "self" becomes
a shadow, a perverse parody of self as it was originally
created. Like Lucifer, or Milton's Satan, longing to be
"himself alone," to be self-willed and self-generative,
he falls into false self-love; he becomes "a motion un-
regenerative" (*Paradise Lost*). His will becomes convo-
luted, and barren; he can only create shadowy parodies,
grotesque imitations of the good.

Sauron is never personified in the book, but appears

only as an eye. That eye is the emblem of false self-
reflexive consciousness. Sauron is the power, a possibility implicit in free will, to turn away from the
whole of creation to the contemplation of self as our
only reality. True self, rightful identity, can only be
found in fellowship. The resolution of the book, the
reunion of the fellowship that has saved the world from
Sauron and made possible *The Return of the King*, depends upon a recognition by each of its members that, as
Shakespeare puts it:

> Then is there mirth in heaven
> When earthly things made even
> Atone together
> (*As You Like It*, V,iv,109-11)

with a pun that makes atonement dependent upon attune-
ment.

The comic/cosmic resolution of the trilogy is Tolkien's answer to the question of how each separate entity, each self, maintains its unique and independent
identity and is yet part of a whole greater than it is.
The answer is not a "blending"; it is only in Mordor
that all creatures are reflections of the One, who is
himself only an eye contemplating its own empty image.
Nor can we live in the Ovidian "golden world" of un-
thinking innocence that is ruled by Tom Bombadil and
Goldberry, the ancestral nature god and goddess, who
nourish our lives as they nourish the perennial lives of
flowers, but who cannot comprehend the burden of self-
conscious individuation that each of us must bear (Tom
Bombadil, as Gandalf tells us, would forget the "One"
Ring, or lose it).

The question, then, is how does a creature atone
"the penalty of Adam." Separated from the world of un-
thinking nature, conscious of self, and forced to act,
how does any "Ring-bearer" maintain the delicate balance
between losing the "One" Ring and falling victim to its
pull? Conceiving of the self as both an entity and a
part, Tolkien tackles the problem of the "guilt of individual existence" as Karl Jaspers defines it: "Guilt
in the larger sense is identical with existence. The
idea, already found in Anaxamander, recurs in Calderon
[and, we might add, in the *Gawain* poet, in Spenser, and
in Shakespeare] although in a different sense — that

man's greatest guilt is to have been born. This is revealed in the fact that my very existence causes misery [as Frodo's existence causes Gollum's].... whether I act or not, merely by existing I infringe upon the existence of others. Passive or active I incur the guilt of existence. A particular life is guilty through its origin."5 And, curiously, Tolkien, like the medieval and Renaissance artists in whose tradition he was working, comes to the same conclusion that was reached by the modern philosopher. The "guilt of individual existence" can only be atoned when it is assumed and when the quest to be relieved of the burden is seen as part of a larger design.

Frodo must assume the burden of the Ring and must journey, not as he first thought from the comfortable, insulated Shire to the boundaries of the familiar world, the Last Homely House only, but beyond that to the very Crack of Doom. He must take that journey, not knowing where it will lead him and never fully aware of its importance in the greater plan, the outcome of which is not understood even by Gandalf the White. His only companion at last is Sam Gamgee, the very emblem of love and service to the other, the agent of *caritas*.

Frodo, the "Ring-bearer" as we are each of us Ring-bearers, is both Everyman and the Hero. His journey is what the medieval commentators upon Virgil called the epic "journey to wisdom." On his journey he must encounter many threats, from the simple desire to "disappear" and forget the demand that has been made of him, to the primal terror of death that he meets in the barrow, to the inferno where he loses his guide to the Balrog — an evil to men more ancient than the moral evil that Sauron represents — to the cave of the terrible Shelob, Tolkien's version of the Black Mother-Goddess of the ancients, to the Crack of Doom. But along the way he also encounters greater and greater manifestations of the healing good — all of them images of fellowship from the initial insistence of Merry and Pippin, creatures like himself, upon risking themselves to accompany him, to the Fellowship of the Nine, creatures of varied natures who are bound by a common cause, to Lothlórien, where Galadriel gives him a glimpse of the larger, cosmic fellowship and the gift of a starlight that cannot fail however deep the present darkness.

At the very end of his journey he is accompanied by
Sam, his simple, loving, "other self," and Gollum, his
darker image, and there he must make a choice that
proves him both good and vulnerable. He has come,
against all odds, to the Crack of Doom. He has fought
the power of the Ring of self to his utmost strength.
But at the end he cannot willingly give it up any more
than Sir Gawain can submit to the Green Knight's axe
stroke without flinching, for the self is our only known
life. It is here, when all that *can* be done has been
done, that Providence intervenes. One strand in Frodo's
destiny, his "unreasonable" charity to Gollum, never
recognized either by him or by us as important, proves
to be his salvation. Just as we cannot know the full
design in which our particular journey is a thread, so
neither can we know the full importance of any step in
the journey until we have come to its end. The quest
has taken place within a larger context. In the "last
battle" all creatures of the Good — from the ents who
bring the most ancient force of life to destroy Saruman's tower of technology, to the Kings of Men, to the
eagles, the horses, and, of course, the heroic hobbits
— must fight Sauron the Dark Lord of the Eye (which is
also the "I") and the whole army of Shadows — shadow
Kings, orcs, who are shadows of elves and dwarves, shadow Riders on shadow distortions that are neither eagles
nor horses, which his power has created to mock and confuse them. Each of the forces of good conquers in the
same way as Frodo, the Ring-bearer, conquers: by meeting
to the best of his ability the demands of the way he has
chosen, preserving his unique integrity, and serving the
needs of the All while never really knowing the whole of
its design.

The many journeys, which are really one journey,
end back in the Shire, for in Tolkien, as in medieval-
Renaissance epic, all journeys end in new beginnings.
But just as each of the travelers has gone through his
particular trial and been transformed, has lost himself
to find himself, so too the Shire must be destroyed
to be rebuilt. It could not remain an Edenic "golden
world." In the literary tradition Troy had to fall
for Rome to be founded, and Britain is Brutus's "second
Rome"; so too the Shire had to fall to become part of
the new Jerusalem, a small but highly honored province
in the territory of the King.

Notes

1. Sidney, *An Apologie for Poesie*, in *English Critical Essays*, ed. E. D. Jones (London, 1963), p. 7.   2. Hugh of St. Victor, *The Didascalion of Hugh of St. Victor*, trans. J. Taylor (New York, 1963), p. 127.   3. *Shakespeare's Ovid, Being Golding's Translation of the Metamorphoses*, ed. W. H. D. Rouse (Carbondale, Ill., 1961).   4. Hollander, *The Untuning of the Sky: Ideas of Music in English Poetry 1500-1700* (Princeton, N.J., 1961), p. 40.   5. Jaspers, *Tragedy Is Not Enough*, tr. Reiche, Moore, and Deutsch (London, 1953), pp. 53, 54.

Daniel Hughes

PIETIES AND GIANT FORMS IN 'THE LORD OF THE RINGS'

No admirer of *The Lord of the Rings* needs to be told
that Tolkien is to be taken seriously, but the range,
the depth, the poetic risk of his accomplishment are,
I think, insufficiently understood. The author's esthetic, as expressed in his essay, "On Fairy-Stories,"
written when the great trilogy was barely under way,
can mislead us — unless we see it as an apologia and a
program of work of the most ambitious kind. Tolkien
allies himself with the Classical against the Romantic
by describing the artistry of the fairy story as "subcreation"; but this perhaps unfortunate formulation
does not imply that artistic activity is an inferior
occupation or that "Fairy-Stories" constitute an inferior genre. By describing his work-to-be as subcreation
and the artist as a subcreator, the author aligns himself with Shaftesbury's eighteenth-century notion of
the artist as "a just Prometheus under Jove" rather than
with Shelley's Tasso-oriented, *"Non merita nome di crea-
tore, se non Iddio ed il Poeta."* But this by no means
suggests that Tolkien does not take the artist or his
creation with anything but complete seriousness. The
Primary Creation is God's work, of course, but, in the
making of "Faërie," which is *not* primarily for children, but for fallen adults, the artist (Tolkien has to
be his own best uncited example) may actually assist in
"the effoliation and multiple enrichment of creation."
Part of his view is familiar enough: the artist is free
to make what he wants, particularly in fairy stories.
"In such 'fantasy,' as it is called, new form is made;
Faërie begins; Man becomes a sub-creator." But note

carefully how seriously Tolkien takes this secondary
act: "An essential power of Faërie is thus the power of
making immediately effective by the will the visions of
'fantasy.' Not all are beautiful or even wholesome, not
at any rate the fantasies of fallen Man.... This aspect
of 'mythology' — sub-creation rather than either representation or symbolic interpretation of the beauties and
terrors of the world — is, I think, too little considered."[1] Although Tolkien is critical of Coleridge in
his essay, surely the famous formulations of the *Biographia Literaria* have influenced him and can help us to
appreciate what has been done in *The Lord of the Rings*.
Coleridge writes of the imagination that "this power,
first put in action *by the will and understanding,* and
retained under their irremissive, though gentle and
unnoticed controul...reveals itself in the balance or
reconciliation of opposite qualities."[2] The will, infected, but capable of redemption, *free to choose,* may
float, may dream, but above all, must construct a conscious vision like the great fantasy-trilogy itself.
Moreover, "fantasy" is the particular goal and product
of subcreation which is superior to either "representation" or "symbolic interpretation." Fantasy in the
form of "narrative art" thus becomes the purest mode of
storytelling; in fact, the finest mode of literary art
itself.

These are large claims, but it is important to understand what Tolkien is *not* doing. His sense of the
term "fantasy" is not limited, he tells us, "to the
queerness of things that have become trite, when they
are suddenly seen from a new angle." This mode, exem-
plified by the preface to the *Lyrical Ballads,* cannot
involve that full creative power which must make and
create the *new.* Again, I think Coleridge can help us.
The Lord of the Rings is a truly imaginative work in the
Coleridgean sense as *The Once and Future King* by T. H.
White, with which it is sometimes compared, is only a
fanciful one, playing with "fixities and definites" that
are plucked from a legend and history only half believed
in. *The Hobbit* is itself, I think, a work of Fancy on
its way to full imaginative confrontations. The trilogy
of the Ring is constantly and organically growing as its
remarkable narrative pace rushes the reader over hesita-
tions into brilliant solutions of form and content. But

what is this "new form" that Tolkien has made and made
available to so many different kinds of readers and re-
sponders? How can a book so thoroughly conversant with
the traditions yet refresh them? Answers to these questions bring us to the human heart of the great work.

The Lord of the Rings is a masterpiece which uses
the forms of irony without an ironic effect. "Subcreation," apart from its relevance to esthetics, reminds us of the great Neo-Christian writer of our
time, Simone Weil, whose grim and moving method of "de-
creation" is ironical, too, a reduction from what we
think we will be to what, in the divine perspective,
we are. Thus, we should come to the Godhead as Shelley
urges himself or his reader to join Adonais,

>   then shrink
> Even to a point within our day and night;
> And keep thy heart light lest it make thee sink
> When hope has kindled hope, and lured thee to the
>   brink.

Or shrink to a hobbit, for he is, essentially, a de-
created human being, both better and less than ourselves. The hobbit is basically a tender parody of
Vitruvian man, but seldom in his trilogy does Tolkien
observe his grand concept as a *transplanted* figure in
the manner of talking horse, wise fox, thoughtful pig;
his conception maintains its integrity throughout in a
context where the grandeur and dignity of being a hobbit, a reduced man, break constantly through. For the
old forms themselves, saga, epic, fable, chronicle,
romance, cannot shine directly for the modern reader.
Tolkien restores these forms by putting the hobbit in
the midst of them, in a mood where the creature is not
overblown to carry an impossible burden nor man lowered
to meet him. The hobbit is the grand *donnée* of this
fantasy, and we must understand how well he *works* before
we can appreciate the unique and special quality of *The
Lord of the Rings*.

We are told that only Gandalf among the Wise has
gone in for hobbit-lore, "an obscure branch of knowledge, but full of surprises" (I,58). Yet hobbits are
neither mysterious nor magical. Their toughness, displayed unconvincingly by Bilbo in *The Hobbit*, but crucial in *The Rings*, is not the expression of superpowers.

Harmlessness is the key to hobbit-essence; their height, between two and four feet; their hairy feet; their shyness; their would-be six meals a day; their feeling for a still-unfallen nature; their lack of interest in history and grand events — all these make them a moving dream of ourselves. Yet, except perhaps in the characterization of Frodo's squire, Sam Gamgee, Tolkien's avoidance of sentimentality is remarkable. He always keeps the hobbit in scale; once we accept the imaginative fact of hobbitry (and if we don't, why read the book at all?), the details of the long fiction follow in perfect order and with unquestionable imaginative coherence.

Coleridge argued that in experiencing *The Tempest* the "principal and only genuine excitement ought to come from within — from the moved and sympathetic imagination."[3] In like manner should we follow the fortunes of the hobbit and his world; there is no other way to approach him. But neither the brilliantly managed conception of the hobbit nor the resources of a learning made new and executed to an astounding richness would bring the trilogy off as more than a don's obsessive winter dream were it not for the success Tolkien has with his hero and central character. In this day when only the antihero seems a viable protagonist in fiction and when the very idea of the hero must be diffused into the archetype and scattered in a thousand faces, the portrait of Frodo Baggins, the Ring-bearer, is a delicate triumph of art and attitude. Frodo, the nephew of Bilbo Baggins, the protagonist of *The Hobbit,* is the unlucky inheritor of the One Ring that must be given back, thrown into the Fire-Mountain in the heart of the evil land of Mordor. The quest is his alone, and only he, Frodo of the peaceful Shire, can perform it.

Frodo is not an "interesting" character, conceived in the round or exhibiting a set of complicated and varied responses. He is that familiar figure at the center of the action, but, as in the case of David Copperfield, it is his goal and the events surrounding his purpose, not his character, that make him the center of attention. The charge that is laid on him is absurd; whereas Bilbo, his predecessor, went to find a treasure, Frodo goes forth to lose one. The consistent sense of renunciation in the central action of the trilogy

heightens the elegiac tone that darkens especially the
third volume, *The Return of the King*. But Frodo, though
a hobbit and distinctly not an elf or one of the Big
Ones, is still, as Bilbo and Gandalf think him, the best
hobbit in the Shire. He is intelligent, courageous, and
true to his quest, even as he is woefully and, it seems,
overpoweringly, beset.

Frodo's despair is illuminated, however, by Simone
Weil's assertion that "we have all...impossible desires
within us as a mark of our destination, and they are
good for us when we no longer hope to accomplish them."[4]
Hope is alleged to die frequently in this fiction, but
such death is not merely a rhetorical device to deepen
the next triumph; neither Frodo nor, I think, his creator understands, in the moment of despair, how hope can
survive, but the true optimism of the work lies in its
confident creative impulsion, always pushing to new
solutions. Frodo's moment of decision at the Council
of Elrond, when he agrees to take the Ring to Mordor, is
not wholly his own; the historical moment of the Shire
folk has come, "when they arise from their quiet fields
to shake the towers and counsels of the great"(I,284);
but he is fully responsible to his choice. There is
never any sense that the dice of his ultimate success
have been loaded.

Frodo's main temptation is to use the Ring to make
himself invisible when his enemies pursue him, although
he requires it less as his danger becomes greater, in
Moria, in Shelob's Lair, in Mordor itself. But the
gradual physical decline of Frodo stands in sharp contrast to the increased height and strength put on by
Merry and Pippin, the hobbit friends who initially accompany him on his quest, but who, in the *ambiance* of
Rohan and Gondor, "grow" and "change" — as Frodo does
not; his wounds are too deep, his purpose too single.
Despite the happy outcome of his quest — the Ring is
thrown into Mount Doom and the Dark Lord Sauron is defeated — he cannot stay in the Shire, but, with Gandalf
and the elven king and queen, must take ship from the
Grey Havens.

To appreciate why Frodo's voyage out is so moving,
even to the point of tragic tears, is to come closer to
the human meaning of the hobbit image itself. Frodo
does not die like the tragic hero, but he is nonetheless

transported to another dimension where he can no longer
truly be a hobbit. Frodo of the Shire is all our understanding of him, but the careful avoidance of the special, the magical, in that knowledge is overthrown by
the hero's translation to exactly that realm Tolkien has
presented so splendidly *apart* from, if *along with,* the
hobbit in the fiction. Frodo's "death" is moving because the hobbit in ourselves must meet a new dispensation. Losing him, we are back in the mimetic world of
fustian heroes on the one hand and fanciful Little
People on the other, and not all the rich and complicated appendixes in the world can soothe us for Frodo's
suffering and departure. The mood is unmistakable: "Go,
bid the soldiers shoot."

There are two other personages in *The Lord of the
Rings* whose presence manifests almost as well as Frodo's
the precision and delicately wrought poise of Tolkien's
intentions: the dreadful Gollum, a parody of Frodo who
yet performs a crucial act, and the wizard Gandalf, an
essential mediating figure between the worlds of the
fantasy. Gollum, the obsessed water-creature driven mad
by his erstwhile possession of the Ring, as demonic as
Frodo is an apocalyptic focus of energy, that loathsome
being who, at the crucial moment, falls into Mount Doom
with the Ring he has bitten from Frodo's finger — Gollum
is one of the imaginative triumphs of the book. This
figure is interesting in himself; his speech, "What has
it got in its pocketses," (*H*,p.95) is the most memorable
and immediately detachable part of the earlier book, but
the "fun" one may have with Gollum, so called for his
gurgling throat, should not obscure his larger meaning
in the fiction. Gandalf predicts that Gollum, whose
initial recovery of the Ring is the key plot device that
brings hobbit and Ring together, will have something to
do before the end (I,269); and the fact is, of course,
that even Gollum is redeemed, in his extinction saving
what we have come to call the "civilized world." Gandalf tells Frodo that Gollum's people were "of hobbit-
kind" (I,62), though surely of a downward-looking type!
When Sam Gamgee helps Frodo to trap Gollum in Book Four,
he is startled to find a resemblance between his master
and the grotesque creature; they are in some way akin,
and, of course, their kinship is their concern with the
Ring, Gollum to repossess it, Frodo to destroy it in the

manner decreed by the Council of Elrond. But they understand each other; the process by which Frodo comes
to pity Gollum, as Bilbo had before him, is an exact
measure of Frodo's mastery over himself as well as over
the terrible power of the Ring. Gollum, the anti-Frodo,
completes our picture of the book's courageous hero.
Together, Frodo and Gollum form one of the most convincing pictures of obsession, how it is fought, and how it
is yielded to, in all fiction.

The presence of the wizard Gandalf poses, I think,
the most difficult technical problem faced in the trilogy, one not completely solved. The wizard, like the
hobbit and many of the other characters in the work,
must be transformed to a greater strength and dignity —
the passage from Gandalf the Grey to Gandalf the White
marking one of the most important metamorphoses in *The
Lord of the Rings*. Gandalf begins in *The Hobbit,* and in
the opening pages of the later work, as a figure of Fancy, semicomical, a bit fuddled as though his creator is
somewhat uncertain about what he should do with him. If
Gandalf becomes too competent, too able to control the
action, too ready a *deus ex machina,* his character will
limit the imaginative possibilities of hobbits and men
too much. In fact, Pippin's cry at the siege of Gondor
— "Gandalf, can't you do something?" — must have been as
frequent a temptation for the fabulist as it is a too-
simple recourse for hobbit and reader. Gandalf is kept
away from the plot for long stretches; he goes away in
Book One, chapter four, not to return until Book Two,
when, in a startling development, he disappears into the
depths of Moria as he battles the monster Balrog; he
then returns mysteriously in chapter five of Book Three,
having undergone his great secret battle alone in the
depths and on the mountain, for the rest of the work not
only interpreter and guide, but a great Wizard Warrior,
Gandalf the White, girded with the sword Glamdring and
commanding his superb horse, Shadowfax. Yet the recognizable archetype of withdrawal and return cannot be
used to explain the Gandalfian mystery. The extent of
Gandalf's power remains unclear until the scene in Book
Three, chapter ten, in which Gandalf confronts his alter
ego, the fallen wizard, Saruman, once his superior, but
now so hopelessly infected by the power of the Dark Lord
that he seeks the One Ring for himself. Gandalf-Saruman

is a pairing like Frodo-Gollum in which the lesser figure's lapse into madness helps to define the strengths,
as well as the weaknesses, of the stronger. Like the
hobbits, we have first admired Gandalf for his fire-
works, the products of Fancy, but we have come to understand how deeply conceived a catalytic agent he really
is in the fiction. Like Frodo, he finally sets sail
from the Grey Havens because his role in historical time
has ended, but it is good that he is on board; Frodo is
not alone.

I have argued that the hobbit is neither mysterious
nor magical; in fact, the central world of the novel,
whether on the hobbit or heroic plane, maintains its own
rational order and odd restraint. Yet the unpredictable
reach of an imagination *not* balanced by form but extended beyond plot and narrative — an essential element in
Tolkien's success — focuses on those figures who stand
to one side of Frodo's quest: Tom Bombadil, the Pan of
Middle-earth; Treebeard, the ent who embodies the spirit
of trees; and, of course, the elves who frame, but do
not constrict, the deepest inner and outer worlds of *The
Lord of the Rings*. These characters point to a freedom
the author cannot allow his main figures. We respond to
them in their detachment, engendered as it is, I think,
by the purity of motive exhibited in the creation of
the hobbit himself. Simone Weil has argued: "On God's
part creation is not an act of self-expansion but of
restraint and renunciation."[5] In literature, the artist (here, the fantasist, in Tolkien's term, the sub-
creator) is God, and I insist, blasphemously perhaps,
that the restraint and renunciation required of an author in choosing the lowly hobbit to bear the burden of
his large narrative enables him to people his creation
with the most convincing men and women of faerie I have
ever encountered. Tom Bombadil, who affects the action
the least, is innocent, prelapsarian Nature, not a Noble
Savage, but that timeless being, joyous in the woods, to
whom the horrendous events of the Third Age of Middle-
earth can have little meaning. He is even impervious to
the power of the Ring, for when Frodo puts it on, Tom
can still see him. At the same time, as Gandalf warns,
Tom Bombadil stands outside the cataclysmic events of
the Third Age and cannot be called upon for help; he has
withdrawn to his own limits and will not come forward

until there is "a change of days." But Treebeard, the
ent, a kind of Tree-Man — slow-moving, thoughtful, im-
memorial — unlike Bombadil, does participate in the wars
against Sauron; Merry and Pippin inspire him to call the
Entmoot at which the decision is made to march on and
destroy Isengard, Saruman's retreat. The ent is one of
Tolkien's happiest inventions, an image reminiscent of
Hopkins and Wordsworth in those poems of fierce attach-
ment to a natural world whose inscapes are threatened
with destruction. Pathos too surrounds Treebeard because the entwives have been missing for many years so
there can be no entings. How long, Tolkien asks in Bombadil and Treebeard, can nature, which we so mishandle,
survive as pure natural song or leaf?

The elves are the very presence of grace in *The Lord
of the Rings,* the boundary of imaginative possibility;
they must be taken with complete seriousness, but in a
different tonality than the hobbits themselves. Nostalgia and remorse surround their natures because they have
been moving west out of the Grey Havens for many years:
an intimation that we, as men, are seeing them for the
last time that contributes strongly to the subtle sense
of loss as the book both darkens and lightens its meanings. In "On Fairy-Stories," Tolkien speaks of "a kind
of elvish craft" by which the Secondary World built up
in Fantasy will engender Secondary Belief in its existence, so we must assume that he believes in elves as he
believes in hobbits. One of the elves, Legolas, becomes
part of the Fellowship of the Ring, and his soothing and
superior presence on the journey from Rivendell, his
stamina and bowmanship, his courtly and lyrical manner
strengthen and dignify the quest, even as they set him
apart from the others. But it is the two great chapters
of Book Two, "Lothlórien" and "The Mirror of Galadriel,"
that best exhibit the role of the elves in the trilogy.
Lórien is an earthly paradise where the elves bide their
time, ruled by the elven-king Celeborn and his lady
Galadriel. Tolkien is precise in his arrangement: in
Rivendell, where the Council of Elrond takes place,
there is a *memory* of ancient things, but in Lórien, the
doomed elven world of the present, the ancient things
live on in the waking world. There is no stain in
Lórien, it is true, but even here, in its most perfect
setting, the work's note of pathos, of loss can be

heard. If Frodo fails, Lórien will be at the mercy of
Sauron the Dark Lord; but, even if he succeeds, the
power of Lórien will be diminished because such triumph
will signify the end of the Third Age when the elves
must depart for the West and the Grey Havens — as they
do. But the elves are not basically presences of sorrow. They offer the strongest joy the imagination can
bring, beyond and above our world. Early on, as Frodo,
Pippin, and Merry start their marvelous journey, the
true elven note is struck, never to be forgotten by the
wanderers; the reader tunes his ears: "Away high in the
East swung Remmirath, the Netted Stars, and slowly above
the mists red Borgil rose, glowing like a jewel of fire.
Then by some shift of airs all the mist was drawn away
like a veil, and there leaned up, as he climbed over the
rim of the world, the Swordsman of the Sky, Menelvagor
with his shining belt. The Elves all burst into song"
(I,91).
      I have yet to examine what for many readers may be
the most striking feat of *The Lord of the Rings*: its
resuscitation of the Heroic Age, its virtues and valors
intact. Most of us read Homer today, probably in Rich-
mond Lattimore's fine translation, without much insight
or interest in the heroic and epic materials in themselves. Tolkien, in writing for *now*, even through his
removed world, has succeeded in doing what might have
been thought impossible in our ostensibly liberal-
democratic, war-hating times; he has almost brought off
an epic as grand as *Beowulf,* as detailed as an old dim
chronicle, and as old-fashioned in its values as an
Icelandic saga or Sir Walter Scott. The internal creative process of the book, as organic as any Coleridgean
plant, comes to flower nowhere more dynamically than
in the presentation of the wars of the Ring, whether
Tolkien is relating the stately muster of Rohan or the
startling account of the siege of Gondor. But these
could not come to pass, I think, without the swelling,
growing role of Aragorn, whose passage from anonymous
Ranger (called Strider) to the grand restored king of
Gondor and the fulfillment of the line of the Númenoreans is the central event of the "external" and "historical" part of the work as the quest of Frodo is crucial
to its "private" and "personal" side. In his introductory note to the reprinting of "On Fairy-Stories"

Tolkien admits that when he and the hobbits got to Bree
in Book One, chapter two, he had no idea who Strider
was, that cloaked and possibly sinister figure who is
very curious about the hobbits and their appearance in
a hostelry so far from the Shire. It is exactly here,
I submit, when the author discovers who Strider is and
what he wants to do with him that *The Lord of the Rings*
starts to assume its large but never baggy shape. Strider is the image that enables Tolkien, the artist,
fantasist, and theorist of faerie, to join hands with
Tolkien the admirer of the Heroic Age's tales and devices. The extraordinary excitement surrounding the
figure of Aragorn as it develops almost tilts the balance of the book, nearly takes it too far from the hobbit, especially in the later scenes in Gondor. But the
mediating presence of Gandalf and the roles of the minor
hobbits, Merry with the Riders of Rohan, Pippin with the
besieged men of Gondor, keep the imaginative proportions
in place, though certainly we have moved very far from
that erstwhile children's book that launched the whole
creative enterprise.

With the breaking of the fellowship that closes Book
Two, the remaining four books of the trilogy divide precisely into two parts, Books Three and Five belonging to
the Heroic Age, Books Four and Six to the theme of the
quest, with the middle pages of Six bringing the two
parts together again when the eagles sent by Gandalf
rescue Frodo and Sam from exploding Mount Doom. (The
last three chapters, modeled on the return of Odysseus,
extend the book more than is necessary perhaps; we know
the Third Age is coming to an end and sense Frodo will
have to depart before he actually goes.) The communal
splendor of Books Three and Five is carefully placed
against the agonizing progress of Frodo to Mordor in
Four and Six, although there is never a sense that the
book has split in two because we never forget that Frodo's approach is made grander by the gathering armies
in the background. It's interesting to note that Tolkien tells us that he wrote Book Three and part of Book
Five before he began Book Four, as though delaying to
gird himself for his hero's worst moment; indeed, Book
Four, with the wounding and apparent death of Frodo,
marks the lowest descent of the author's vision. But
the successful campaign against Saruman in Book Three

and the breaking of the Siege of Gondor in Book Five
hint at the possible incredible resolution of Frodo's
mission. The hobbits have their place indeed in the
grand events of these days. The heinous captain of the
Ringwraiths is slain by the lady Éowyn and the hobbit
Merry when, in avenging their fallen King Théoden, the
hobbit, who has not had much status in the work, stabs
his enemy from behind, thus bringing together heroic
confrontation and hobbit guile. The death of this
dreadful creature demonstrates the true nature of the
demons in Tolkien's world; his hauberk and mantle become
immediately empty and his cry, bodiless and thin, "was
never heard again in that age of this world" (III,117).
And Meriadoc Brandybuck takes his place among the great
warriors of the ages.

    There is some truth in the complaint voiced by a few
critics that the Opposition in *The Lord of the Rings* is
too simply conceived. Although as a Christian optimist
Tolkien believes in heroism and the rise of the lowly,
his orcs, the general troops of evil in the book, are
creepy-crawly figures more akin to the sadistic small
horrors glimpsed in the corner of Fra Angelico than they
are to the powerful, embodied visions of Dante. But the
larger set pieces of demonic confrontation in the book
— the Balrog who disappears with Gandalf into Moria, the
noisome Shelob who terrorizes Sam and Frodo in the tunnel leading to Mordor — these are impressive figures of
nightmare. Like Blake, whose engravings present few
visually impressive images of the demonic, Tolkien would
not dwell on the beasties themselves, but on the mental
strife of the would-be Christians who are trying to wake
from Error. His finest decision in this regard is surely his keeping Sauron, the Dark Lord of the Rings, off
the center of his stage except as a powerful Roving Eye
whose presence is felt everywhere but whose direct specific embodiment is not required. Besides, we get our
direct encounter with Evil in Saruman's Tower of Orthanc
in Book Three; a frontal attack on Barad-dûr, Sauron's
tower, could be only repetitious. Indeed, Saruman is
like Blake's Urizen because Isengard under his direction
has become a place of heartless machines and wheels.
Just as Urizen yields to the less concrete but more
terrible figure of Satan in the Prophetic Books, so Saruman, a figure unable to contain the deeper disorder

required for the full working out of the drama of the
quest, must be replaced by Sauron whose *essence* must be
dealt with in the apocalyptic moment of the Third Age of
Middle-earth. The Heroic Age does not require rounded
villains — Tolkien has the tradition too firmly in hand
to require them; and the quest theme is, as I have said,
a renunciation, a surrender. Noble villains not needed.
   The energy displayed in all these matters, the hobbit and the Heroic Age, the quest and its nightmares,
comes to no more splendid expression than in the best
poem of the many in the work, a successful recreation of
Anglo-Saxon verse in its own right, but in its context,
following the death of Théoden, King of Rohan, while
Frodo somewhere, somehow, struggles toward Mount Doom,
an overpoweringly moving and splendid moment. The shining piety and the deep imaginative strength of the book
flash forth from the full orchestra.

> We heard of the horns in the hills ringing,
> the swords shining in the South-kingdom.
> Steeds went striding to the Stoningland
> as wind in che morning. War was kindled.
> There Théoden fell, Thengling mighty,
> to his golden halls and green pastures
> in the Northern fields never returning,
> high lord of the host. Harding and Guthláf,
> Dúnhere and Déorwine, doughty Grimbold,
> Herefara and Herubrand, Horn and Fastred,
> fought and fell there in a far country:
> in the Mounds of Mundburg under mould they lie
> with their league-fellows, lords of Gondor.
> Neither Hirluin the Fair to the hills by the sea,
> nor Forlong the old to the flowering vales
> ever, to Arnach, to his own country
> returned in triumph; nor the tall bowmen,
> Derufin and Duilin, to their dark waters,
> meres of Morthond under mountain-shadows.
> Death in the morning and at day's ending
> lords took and lowly. Long now they sleep
> under grass in Gondor by the Great River.
> Grey now as tears, gleaming silver,
> red then it rolled, roaring water:
> foam dyed with blood flamed at sunset;
> as beacons mountains burned at evening;
> red fell the dew in Rammas Echor. (III,124-25)

Though *The Lord of the Rings* is predicated on classical assumptions, and a classical esthetic, it reminds
us more of Romantic poetry — of Blake in its search for
restored methods and images; of Wordsworth in its pieties and tones. When Blake writes jauntily in the preface to *Jerusalem* that he is again "displaying his Giant
forms to the public," we smile, knowing how small an
audience he had and understanding that his forms are
only now finding their public through collective labors
nearly equal to the intensity of the forms themselves.
I am not suggesting that the popular *Lord of the Rings*
is equal in density or subtlety to the Prophetic Books,
but it moves in that direction by refusing to be allegory, or representational in the low mimetic sense of
that term. Like Blake, Tolkien distrusts allegory because he seeks the detached experience of what he calls
"sub-creation" which we, in seeking to purge the term
of any false connotations, may better understand by
Geoffrey Hartman's "Pure Representation" in which "the
poet represents the mind as knowing without a cause from
perception."[6] We cannot perceive a hobbit, but we can
imagine one, *without* resemblances or assemblings from
the known world. Attempts to allegorize the trilogy
from World War I or II can only limit, even demean, what
has been accomplished. Of course, as Tolkien admits,
the loss of his friends in the first war might have had
something to do with his personal feelings in his book,
and I think the threat of Nazism is somewhere in its
propulsive stirrings. But — horrors! — Sauron is not
Hitler, nor Frodo Winston Churchill. The giant forms
of Tolkien's world, however, do not show the psychic and
archetypal energies of Blake's creations; they are — we
have known it all the time — the great modes and methods
of English literature itself which here, indirectly,
finds one of its finest tributes. The trilogy is a triumph and riot of a deep traditional learning well lived
and well wrought.

Tolkien's tone is not very Blakean; it is basically
pious, pious of English letters and the English country-
side, pious in its observation of man's place in a hostile world where he must make his way. Somewhere between Dickens and Wordsworth, particularly the latter,
The Lord of the Rings finds its refreshened tonalities.
The Heroic Age, "Milton, thou shouldst be living at this
hour!" and the private quest (compare the "unfathered

vapour" of Imagination in *The Prelude)* come together
in what Wordsworth hoped would be a poetry of healing
and "recompense."   So in Tolkien joy may live and new
forms arise.   "On Fairy-Stories" concludes: "All tales
may come true; and yet, at the last, redeemed, they may
be as like and as unlike the forms that we give them
as Man, finally redeemed, will be like and unlike the
fallen that we know."

Notes

1. "On Fairy-Stories," pp. 22f.   2. *Biographia Literaria,* ed.
J. Shawcross (Oxford, 1907), II, 12 (my italics).   3. *Coleridge's Essays and Lectures on Shakespeare* (London, 1911), p.
66.   4. Weil, *Waiting for God* (New York, 1951), p. 126).
5. Ibid., p. 145.
    6. Hartman, *The Unmediated Vision* (New York, 1966), p. 128.

Patrick Grant

TOLKIEN: ARCHETYPE AND WORD

The Lord of the Rings embodies an inherent morality,
which derives largely from the traditions of Christian
and epic poetry. Yet the trilogy is not explicitly
religious and is neither allegorical nor doctrinal.
Tolkien well knows that the Dantesque form of Christian
epic, wherein history effortlessly assumes the framework
of dogma, cannot be successfully imitated in post-
Romantic times. In Milton's *Paradise Lost* the sacramentalism fundamental to Dante's vision is already
transformed. For Milton, subjective experience, not
a doctrinal formula of words, is the key to faith, and
medieval "realism," which assumes the participation of
words in the extramental reality they signify, is not
part of the consciousness that produced *Paradise Lost*.
   What remain in Milton are, in generalized form, the
great themes of the Christian epic: first, and most important, that true heroism is spiritual; also, that love
is obedience and involves freedom; that faith and hope
are based on charity; that Providence directs the affairs of the world. The reader is repeatedly challenged
to establish an attitude to these issues, and the vast
shifts of time and space — heavenly, infernal, past,
future, prelapsarian, postlapsarian — are means of
pressing the challenge upon his attention. In no other
Christian poem does the real (inner) meaning so ener-
getically parody the canonical orthodoxies of the external form.
   By the time of Blake (who, significantly, saw Milton
as a noble spirit except for his doctrine) the "paradise
within" has found expression in language even further

removed from canonical orthodoxy than Milton's. The Romantics primarily inherit Blake's vision, and so, basically, does Tolkien, essentially a post-Romantic like
his friends C. S. Lewis, Owen Barfield, and Charles
Williams. One consequence is that the principles of
Christian epic are experienced in Tolkien not explicitly
but as embodied themes, a map of values as in *Paradise
Lost,* and without the traditional dogmatic theology that
Milton's great poem is already in process of casting
off. The trilogy is, significantly, set in the essentially inner realm of faerie, close to the world of
dream and myth, where, Tolkien tells us, "primordial
human desires" are met and interpreted.[1]

The archetypal flavor of Tolkien's description of
faerie, together with his dreamlike settings in Middle-
earth, have readily evoked among critics the language
and thought of Jung, and, in a historical context, Jung
is certainly a prime explicator in the twentieth century
of the "interiorization" of spiritual experience so
characteristic of post-Romantic religion. In this respect the psychoanalyst complements the writer of fairy
stories. *The Lord of the Rings* can be read with surprising consistency as an interior journey through the
psyche as Jung describes it, and archetypal structures
in the trilogy will be a central concern of this essay.
Yet I wish to establish from the outset that a purely
Jungian approach has limitations, for Tolkien at all
times evaluates the archetypes, however implicitly, in
light of the literary conventions of Christian epic.
The Word, in a Christian sense, is a primary archetype
which both spiritualizes and revalidates for man the extramental world of history and material extension. Only
in carefully observed physical reality can the subcreation of faerie achieve its real enchantment, and open
into the truth which Tolkien describes, in the old language, as Eucharistic.[2] The great pains taken with the
historical background to Middle-earth are not without
point. They save the book from becoming allegory, or a
thin fantasy of "interior space," and in his "Eucharistic" view of history and of the Word, Tolkien addresses
again the key problems of the Christian epic in modern
times: the possibilities of sacramentalism, and the relation of the archetypes of inner vision to Christian
ordinances and heroic themes.

The group of friends to whom Tolkien first read *The
Lord of the Rings*, the Inklings, found Jung temperamen-
tally attractive, though they regarded him also with a
certain suspicion. C. S. Lewis avows that he is "enchanted" by Jung, and has, on occasion, "slipped into"
a Jungian manner of criticism.[3] He admits that Maud
Bodkin, the pioneer critic of Jungian archetypal patterns in literature, exerted considerable influence on
him. Owen Barfield praises Jung for understanding the
spiritual nature of consciousness and its evolution: the
Jungian "collective unconscious" and appeal to myth are
much-needed antidotes to twentieth-century materialism
which threatens to make an object of man himself.[4] On
the negative side, Lewis thinks that Jung's explanation
of "primordial images" itself awakens a primordial image
of the first water, while Barfield feels that in Jung
the "Spiritual Hierarchies" have withdrawn from the
world, and exist, interiorized, within the individual
will and too much cut off from the extramental world.[5]
    It is important not to put the words of Lewis and
Barfield into Tolkien's mouth (he was as difficult to
influence as a bandersnatch, according to Lewis),[6] yet
Tolkien at least shared the interests and temperament of
his friends. Certainly the reader of his essay on fairy
stories cannot easily avoid the Jungian flavor of several of Tolkien's key theories. He describes faerie in
relation to dream, stating that in both "strange powers
of the mind may be unlocked" (p.13). He talks of the
encounter in fairy stories with "certain primordial human desires" (p.13), and claims the stories are "plainly
not primarily concerned with possibility, but with de-
sirability" (p.40). He talks of a "Cauldron of Story"
which waits "for the great figures of Myth and History"
(p.29). These are added like fresh pieces to a stock
which has been simmering from the beginnings of storytelling — that is, from the beginnings of the human mind
itself. In the essay on *Beowulf*, Tolkien especially
appreciates the balance and "opposition of ends and beginnings," the progress from youth to old age in the
hero, and the satisfaction that comes from perceiving
the "rising and setting" of a life.[7]
    We can easily enough feel here the typical Jung-
ian insistence on dream and fantasy, the theory of a
collective unconscious which (like Tolkien's cauldron)

contains archetypes stirred into activity by the artist, and the theory of transformation in the individual
psyche, whereby beginnings and ends are balanced in a
successful human life. But more important, Tolkien's
theory finds full embodiment in *The Lord of the Rings*.
The trilogy is set in faerie, in this case the imaginary
world of Middle-earth, at a time near the beginnings of
man's ascendance in the history of the world. Middle-
earth is often dreamlike: a world of shifting contours
and of magic, of nightmarish fear and exquisite ethereal
beauty. Helpful and treacherous creatures work for the
powers of good and evil, and landscapes become sentient
embodiments of human fears and desires. It is a short
step to the appearance of nature spirits, like Tom Bombadil, or to the magic of the elves, and, as we move
closer to those who possess more than human wisdom and
power, the contours of time and space themselves begin
to blur. Although controlled by the narrative art and
by basic structural oppositions such as those between
light and dark, good and evil, the story moves basically
in a world where forms and images blend and flow and interpenetrate, and where the eye of the beholder determines fear and terror, beauty and glory. All this has
the very quality of that "interior space" that Barfield
names as Jung's special province.[8]
     For Jung, certainly, fairy stories and dreams are
characteristically inhabited by helpful and treacherous
animals and monsters, and landscapes, especially when
they involve woods and mountains, are favorite representations of the unconscious.[9] Jung also talks of a common figure, the "vegetation numen," king of the forest,
who is associated with wood and water in a manner that
recalls Tom Bombadil. Magic too is important, and Jung
explains that "the concentration and tension of psychic
forces have something about them which always looks like
magic." He stresses also a "contamination" of images,
by which he means a tendency to overflow contours — "a
melting down of images."[10] This, says Jung, may look
like distortion and can be terrifying, but it can also
be a process of assimilation and a source of great beauty and inspiration. His perception applies precisely to
the viewpoint technique of *The Lord of the Rings*. Jung
also points to certain characteristic formal elements
in dreams and fairy stories, such as "duality," "the

opposition of light and dark," and "rotation (circle, sphere),"[11] but insists that they should not be considered apart from the complex flowing energy of the psyche. Moral choices are not simply a matter of black or white. Jung stresses "the bewildering play of antinomies"[12] which contribute to higher awareness. Good may be produced by evil, and possibly lead to it. This process, which Jung calls "enantiodromia,"[13] is of central importance in the art of Tolkien: a broad opposition of light and dark, and of good and evil, becomes confused in the trilogy as we enter the minds of individuals in process of finding their way on the quest. Though Gollum hates light and loves shade, Frodo's relation to Gollum is extremely complex, and throughout the trilogy the minds of the men in particular are continually ambivalent.

That Jung and Tolkien isolate such similar motifs from fairy stories, dreams, fantasy, and myth, is hardly surprising, but in *The Lord of the Rings* the inner drama corresponds also with particular fidelity to the details of the psychic process Jung calls "individuation." This is, basically, the "realization of the whole man" achieved in a balanced and fulfilled life when consciousness and the unconscious are linked together in a living relation. The process involves a journey to the self, which Jung describes as not only the center of a person's psyche but also the circumference that embraces both conscious and unconscious.[14] Characteristically, the self is represented in dreams and mythology as a mandala — a square within a circle, or circle within a square, or in figures that are spherical, representing wholeness.

Jung insists that individuation, or selfhood, is not mere ego-consciousness. As the shortsighted ego responds to the demands of inner growth, the way to the self is indicated by representations of archetypes, those primordial and recurring images in human experience which express the basic structures of the psyche, and which become increasingly numinous, impressive, and dangerous as they emerge from the deeper levels of the unconscious. First and nearest to the surface, so that we can become aware of it by reflection, is the shadow. The shadow is the *"personal unconscious,"* and, among the archetypes, is the "easiest to experience."[15] It repre-

sents the elements a person represses as incompatible
with his chosen ideal — "for instance, inferior traits
of character and other incompatible tendencies."[16] The
shadow is ambiguous — it contains morally reprehensible
tendencies, but can also display good qualities, such as
normal instincts that have been repressed but are necessary to consciousness. In dreams it is represented as
a figure of the same sex as the dreamer, and, in accord
with its ambiguous status, may be either a threat that
follows him, or a guide.

Further from consciousness is the anima/animus archetype. This is a representation of the feminine side
of a man's unconscious, or the masculine side of a woman's. The anima (the more important for Tolkien) is,
like the shadow, ambivalent. She is both the nourishing
and the destructive mother. On the one hand she is
Dante's Beatrice, the Virgin Mary, the Muses who inspire
man to create, the dream girl of popular fantasy and
song. On the other hand she is a witch, poisonous and
malevolent, or a Siren who, however beautiful, lures a
man to his death and destruction. For Jung, "the animus and the anima should function as a bridge, or a
door, leading to the images of the collective unconscious."[17]

More profound, and often presented with the anima as
friend or protector, is the archetype of the hero. He
is often represented in a dangerous situation or on a
difficult quest, the anticipation of the individuation
process, an approach to wholeness. The hero often has
an aura of the supernatural, which offsets his vulnerability, another essential trait, for he is both semidivine and a child. "This paradox...runs through his
whole destiny like a red thread. He can cope with the
greatest perils, yet, in the end, something quite insig-
nificant is his undoing."[18] The hero archetype is often
accompanied by the strange and numinous: "dragons, helpful animals, and demons; also the Wise Old Man...all
things which in no way touch the boundaries of everyday.
The reason for this is that they have to do with the
realization of a part of the personality which has not
yet come into existence but is still in the process of
becoming."[19]

The deepest archetype on the journey towards the
self is the figure of the Wise Old Man, a helpful figure

who, when the hero is in a hopeless situation, can ex-
tricate him. He is magician, guru, a personification
of wisdom. He seems not to be bound by time, and he is
strongly endowed with numinous power — for instance,
magic. Also, "apart from his cleverness, wisdom, and
insight," the Wise Old Man is "notable for his moral
qualities."[20] But along with the other archetypes he
is also an ambivalent figure, like Merlin, in whom the
enantiodromia of good and evil can appear most paradoxically.

In *The Lord of the Rings* the theme of a quest in-
volving a ring, symbol of binding and wholeness which
must be preserved from the powers of darkness and evil
by the powers of light and goodness, suggests the beginnings of a typical journey towards individuation: the
promise of a "true conjunctio" which involves the threat
of dissolution, or "false conjunctio." Frodo, at the
beginning, is childlike and must endure the terrors of
monsters, dragons, and the underworld. Aragorn, his
companion, who likewise undergoes such trials, is of
strange and royal origins, protector of a noble lineage,
and a semidivine figure with the magic power of healing.
Frodo and Aragorn represent different aspects of the
hero — Frodo his childlike quality, Aragorn his nobility
and power; and each must support and learn from the
other. The hobbit, for good reason as we shall see,
receives foremost attention, and the story is in a special sense his. As it proceeds, Frodo more and more
puts off the childlike ways of the Shire and assumes the
lineaments of heroism, acquiring, at the end, a truly
numinous quality. Moreover, as his understanding deep-
ens, Frodo moves through a process equivalent to Jung's
individuation, which is charted by the main action of
the book. He encounters the shadow (Gollum), anima
(Galadriel), and Wise Old Man (Gandalf). Each archetype
has a good and bad side, the good leading to understanding and fellowship, the bad to death, isolation, and the
loss of identity or self. So Galadriel is contrasted
with Shelob, the heroes with the Ringwraiths, and Gandalf with the evil magician Saruman. Gollum is, by
nature, ambivalent. He is the shadow, or personal unconscious, and we will deal with him first.

At the beginning Frodo does not realize his shadow
personality; he does not know that he is being pursued

by Gollum. He knows only a vaguely uncomfortable
feeling that increases as the story develops. As the
fellowship sets out for Lothlórien, Frodo "had heard
something, or thought he had. As soon as the shadows
had fallen about them and the road behind was dim, he
had heard again the quick patter of feet" (I,351). The
others do not notice. Soon after, Frodo is startled by
"a shadowy figure," which "slipped round the trunk of
the tree and vanished" (I,360). Again, he alone sees
Gollum who has been pursuing the Ring, moving in the
dark because he fears light.

Significantly, Gollum is of the same race and sex as
Frodo, as is appropriate for a shadow figure. He is a
hobbit, fallen into the power of the Ring and debased to
a froglike, emaciated, underground creature of primitive
cunning and instinct. He is clearly a threat which Frodo must learn to acknowledge as a potentiality in his
own being. To ignore the shadow, as Jung indicates, is
to risk inflation of the ego.[21] The relationship between Frodo and the repulsive Gollum therefore must become one of mutual acknowledgment. Sam, to his own con-
sternation, sees the peculiar link between the two: they
"were in some way akin and not alien: they could reach
one another's minds" (II,225). So Frodo insists on un-
binding Gollum and trusting his promise, and the shadow,
ever ambivalent, becomes a guide without ceasing to be
dangerous. Gollum leads Frodo to Shelob's lair, but he
also saves him at the last moment from a fatal inflation
of pride which would constitute the failure of the
quest: "But for him, Sam, I could not have destroyed the
Ring.... So let us forgive him!" (III,225).

Frodo has confronted Gollum before the party arrives
at Lothlórien, but only after the encounter with Galadriel can he bind and release the shadow. The meeting
with Galadriel is an overwhelming experience for the
entire company, not just for Frodo. Although she deals
more with him than with the others, she is not bound to
Frodo in the particular way that Gollum is. Her significance has less to do with the personal unconscious than
with the collective unconscious. She is a striking representative of the anima, a figure which, Jung says, is
often "fairy like" or "Elfin,"[22] and Galadriel is, indeed, an elf. She is also a bridge to the deeper elements of the psyche, and can reveal hidden elements in

the souls of the company. "None save Legolas and Aragorn could long endure her glance" (I,372), and she
shows to each one the dangers of the quest and the personal weakness he brings to it. In her mirror she shows
to Frodo the larger history in which he is involved, and
he responds with awe and terror. The numinous power
characteristic of the anima almost overwhelms him, so
that he even offers her the Ring. Galadriel replies in
words that clearly indicate the dangers of fixation on
the anima and warn of her destructive aspect: "You will
give me the Ring freely! In place of the Dark Lord you
will set up a Queen. And I shall not be dark, but beautiful and terrible as the Morning and the Night.... All
shall love me and despair!" (I,381). Frodo instead must
use Galadriel's knowledge and wisdom to further the
quest: she is a bridge to the darkness of Mordor, to
which the hero must journey. So Frodo carries with him
the influence of Galadriel's fairylike, timeless, and
magically radiant beauty, and it serves to protect him.
Symbolically, she gives him a phial of light to bear
into the darkness. The light not only shows Frodo the
way, but helps him against the Ringwraiths, and, most
important, enables him to face Shelob.

If Galadriel is the anima in its beneficent aspect,
Shelob the spider-woman is the destructive anima who
poisons to kill. Gollum talks of a mysterious "she" who
may help him win back the Ring, and he means Shelob —
"all living things were her food, and her vomit darkness" (II,332). As Frodo meets her, he holds up the
light: "'Galadriel!' he called, and gathering his courage he lifted up the Phial once more" (II,330). Galadriel's light and Shelob's darkness, the principles of
life and death, of nourishment and destruction, contend
for Frodo who must meet them both — the anima in both
aspects, beneficent and malevolent.

Other anima figures throughout The Lord of the Rings
present an appeal much like Galadriel's. Mainly we
think of Arwen, another elf, whose "loveliness in living
thing Frodo had never seen before nor imagined in his
mind" (I,239). She is destined to marry Aragorn, and
their union represents the "syzygy," the ideal union of
anima and animus. The self is often represented by the
marriage of such a "divine, royal, or otherwise distinguished couple."[23] Less fortunate than Arwen, however,

is Éowyn, whose love for Aragorn cannot be reciprocated, with the result that she becomes the victim of her own animus. When Aragorn leaves her, as he must, Éowyn assumes the disguise of the warrior Dernhelm, who "desired to have nothing, unless a brave death in battle" (III, 242). Éowyn, in Jungian terms, is possessed by the negative animus (often represented as a death-demon) which in this case drives towards suicide. Such a possession often results, says Jung, in "a transformation of personality" which "gives prominence to those traits which are characteristic of the opposite sex."[24] Only through the love of Faramir does Éowyn change — "or else at last she understood it. And suddenly her winter passed, and the sun shone on her" (III,243).

The heroic figures of *The Lord of the Rings* are, as we have said, Aragorn and Frodo. Aragorn is a king in exile, preserver of a noble lineage, who passes through the Paths of the Dead, fights a crucial turn in the epic battle, and proclaims a new dispensation. The hero, as Jung says, is a "greater man...semi-divine by nature," who meets "dangerous adventures and ordeals,"[25] and encounters the Wise Old Man. Significantly, the numinous quality of the semidivine hero is not immediately obvious in Aragorn, who appears first as the Ranger Strider, suspected by the party and by us. Only when we pass more deeply into the quest do we learn of his noble lineage, of his destiny and his power of healing. He grows in our minds in stature as he looks into the magic *palantír,* passes through the Paths of the Dead, and is received, finally, as king. Aragorn is very much the traditional quest hero, but we observe him primarily from the outside.

Frodo, though his birth is peculiar among hobbits, is not a born hero like Aragorn, and we observe him from within, often sharing his point of view. As the story opens, we find in Frodo the vulnerability of the child which, according to Jung, often accompanies the hero's powers. But Frodo gradually develops away from his early naïveté, from the diffident hobbit, wondering why he was chosen and thinking to destroy the Ring with a hammer (I,70). Growth into higher consciousness is painful; yet as Frodo carries the burden, his power increases, and as he passes through the dark experiences that lead to the Council of Elrond, the numinous aura

and magic of the heroic archetype increasingly adhere to
him. He finds he can see more clearly in the dark.   In
Galadriel's mirror he sees the depths of the history in
which he is involved, and he becomes the bearer of the
magic light into the perilous realms. Slowly he acquires wisdom and a nobility comparable to that of Aragorn, so that, as we accompany Frodo's development and
participate in it, we come to understand Aragorn himself
more fully. As the tale ends, Frodo has achieved a heroic sanctity verging on the otherworldly.

The heroes throughout *The Lord of the Rings* are
opposed by the Ringwraiths. As each archetype has a
negative aspect, so the hero, says Jung, is especially
threatened by dissolution "under the impact of the collective forces of the psyche." The characteristic challenge is from "the old, evil power of darkness" which
threatens to overwhelm the hero and the self-identity he
is striving to bring about.[26] The power of Sauron the
Dark Lord is exactly such an old and evil force, and in
The Lord of the Rings his representatives, the negative
counterparts of the heroes, are the Black Riders. The
menace they present balances perfectly the power that
emanates from the heroic Aragorn, while their dissolution in Sauron's old and evil darkness, representing the
loss of self, is indicated by the fact that the Black
Riders have no faces.

The heroes must resist such loss of self and grow
towards wisdom, a spiritual quality represented by the
profound archetype of the Wise Old Man. More mysterious
than the heroes, Gandalf's part in the quest is often
beyond the reach of the story, and his knowledge remains
unfathomable. When we first meet him, he seems more an
old clown than a powerful magician. The interpretation
of wisdom as foolishness is a traditional error of
fools. In this case, it reflects the naïveté of the
comfortable hobbits: Gandalf's "fame in the Shire was
due mainly to his skill with fires, smokes, and lights.
... To them he was just one of the 'attractions' at the
Party" (I,33). But Gandalf, like Aragorn, grows in
stature as we, with Frodo, learn more about him. He is
continually ahead of the quest, exercising a strange,
almost Providential control. He reproves Frodo for many
mistakes and seems to know the whole story in detail,
even though it happened in his absence. "You seem to

know a great deal already" (I,231), says Frodo. We do
not question Gandalf's knowledge, but believe simply
that its source is beyond our ken.

Gandalf also has a knack for appearing when he is
needed. At the ford he sends a flood in the nick of
time as Frodo's will fades. His wisdom leads the armies
to Mordor and circumvents the trap set by the enemy who
possesses Frodo's clothes. His eagles rescue Frodo and
Sam at the last moment, and in the final episode of the
story he makes sure (though we do not know how he knows)
that Merry and Pippin will accompany Sam on his ride
home, after Frodo departs for the Havens: "'For it will
be better to ride back three together than one alone'"
(III,310). Here Gandalf provides, as he does throughout, for the deeper need, and there is a touch of magic
in his actions.

For Jung, the Wise Old Man, as we have seen, appears
especially when the hero is in trouble — "in a situation
where insight, understanding, good advice, determina-
tion, planning, etc., are needed but cannot be mustered
on one's own resources." He often, moreover, adopts
the guise of a magician, and is, essentially, a spirit
archetype. Thus, the Wise Old Man is sometimes a "real"
spirit, namely, the ghost of one dead. Tolkien, interestingly, has described Gandalf as "an angel," and we
are to believe that he really died in the struggle with
the Balrog, reappearing as Gandalf the White, an embodied spirit and a figure of great numinous power.
Also, the Wise Old Man gives the necessary magical tal-
isman, which, in Galdalf's case, is the Ring itself.[27]

The Old Man, however, has a wicked aspect too. Just
as Galadriel has her Shelob, and the heroes their Ringwraiths, so Gandalf has his antitype, the magician Saruman. They meet on equal ground, and between them the
great struggle for self or dissolution of self is once
again fought: "Like, and yet unlike" (II,183), says
Gimli pointedly, as he observes the two at Isengard.
Their contest is based on a symbolism of light: Saruman
is at first white, and Gandalf, a lesser magician, is
gray. But Gandalf becomes white as Saruman falls to the
powers of darkness and his robes become multicolored,
"woven of all colours, and if he moved they shimmered
and changed hue so that the eye was bewildered" (I,
272). Saruman's multicolor, like the facelessness of

the riders, indicates a dissolution of identity. White
is whole; fragmented, it is also dissipated.
    The final and most elusive archetype is that of the
self. Perhaps Tolkien's trilogy as a work of art which
is more than the sum of its parts is the most satisfac-
tory representation of this archetype, for the whole
meaning is activated within the reader, who alone can
experience its completeness. But the most effective me-
diator between the ordinary reader and the "whole" world
of Middle-earth, the character who in the end is closest
to ourselves and who also must return to ordinary life,
is Sam Gamgee. Sam has become, in the process of the
story, Samwise, but he is less removed from ourselves
than Frodo or the other characters. As he leaves, Frodo
says to Sam: "You will have to be one and whole, for
many years. You have so much to enjoy and to be, and to
do" (III,309). The commendation of Sam's wholeness, and
the directive to return to the ordinary world bearing
that wholeness with him, are a directive to the reader:
ripeness is all. But such wisdom as Sam achieves is not
easily come by, as the entire book indicates, and there
is no case for critical denunciation of Tolkien on the
grounds that his hobbits are simplistic or escapist.
The Shire is not a haven, and the burden of the tale is
that there are no havens in a world where evil is a reality. If you think you live in one, you are probably
naïve like the early Frodo, and certainly vulnerable.

    The archetypal patterns we have examined indicate
the extent to which the trilogy can be read as a contemporary exploration of "interior space" analyzed in such
novel terms in this century by Jung. Like Barfield and
Lewis, however, Tolkien assumes a firmer stance before
the archetypes than Jung. Lewis's criticism that Jung
offers a myth to explain a myth can be met only by assertion: there is a myth that is true, and fundamental.
Following such a line of thought, Tolkien insists that
successful fairy stories give a glimpse of truth which
he describes as Eucharistic. The typical "eucatastrophe," the "turn" at the end of a good fairy story, has
the sudden effect of a miraculous grace and gives a
"fleeting glimpse of Joy," a momentary participation in
the state that man most desires.[28] This joy, says Tolkien, is "a sudden glimpse of the underlying reality of

truth" (p. 71). In this sense, the Christian story has "entered History and the primary world," and in it the "desire and aspiration of sub-creation has been raised to the fulfillment of Creation. The birth of Christ is the eucatastrophe of Man's history. The Resurrection is the eucatastrophe of the story of the Incarnation" (pp. 71-72). In Western culture, the Christian story has thus contributed, and also transformed, the Cauldron of Story which Tolkien has discussed earlier in his essay. The basic Christian ingredient substantially alters the flavor of the entire simmering stock.

There are two significant implications in Tolkien's theory. First, the Christian influence on great poetry is profound, particularly on the epic, which addresses itself especially to the values by which men should live. Tolkien's essay on *Beowulf* indicates his appreciation of this fact. Second, the insistence on an ideal Eucharistic participation of the fantasy in the real world leads to a view of art analogous to the Christian Incarnation of the Word. In the greatest story, history and archetype interpenetrate. So in the fairy story, which typically activates the archetypes, historical verisimilitude is of the utmost importance. We must accept that the land of faerie is "true" before it can fully affect us.

The Lord of the Rings, therefore, as a fairy story based on these premises, is more than the inner psychodrama that a purely Jungian interpretation suggests, in which outer object is offset by inner, and in which a fairy tale typically depicts, as Jung says, "the unconscious processes that compensate the Christian, conscious situation."[29] For Tolkien, if it is good, the fairy tale participates in the Christian, conscious situation, and in the primary archetype of the Word made Incarnate from which that Christian consciousness derives. Tolkien faces, therefore, the crucial problem for the Christian writer — the problem faced first by Milton — of formulating a vision in which Christian assertion, history, and imagination can coinhere. For Tolkien, the "paradise within" must, ideally, be raised to fulfillment in the primary world of history, and this implies a sacramental, if nondoctrinal, view of reality. But it does not imply any simple reversion to medievalism: Tolkien does not write allegory, which assumes a

corporate acceptance of dogmatic formulas based on a
"realist" epistemology. The morality of his story is,
as we have seen, implicit. His theory does, however,
help to explain the inordinate pains spent on the appendixes, the background history, the landscape, names,
traditions, annals and the entire sense of a "real
world" of Middle-earth. History and the "Primary World"
are more fully rendered in Tolkien than in Milton, and,
essentially, they mark the difference between a Eucharistic and a nonsacramental view of the world. Yet the
great themes of the Christian epic remain implicit as a
map of values in much the same form in *The Lord of the
Rings* as in *Paradise Lost*. First, and most important,
is the concept of Christian heroism, a spiritual quality
that depends on obedience rather than prowess or personal power. Second, heroism is basic to the meaning of
love. Third, charity, or love, is the foundation of
faith and hope. And last, Providence directs the affairs of the world.

Tolkien first broaches the question of Christian
heroism in the essay on *Beowulf* and in the "ofermod" appendix to *The Homecoming of Beorhtnoth Beorhthelm's Son*.
Echoing a tradition of Christian thought as old as Augustine's *De Doctrina,* Tolkien points out that Beowulf's
fame is "the noble pagan's desire for the *merited praise*
of the noble." Consequently, his "real trust was *in his
own might,*"[30] and Beowulf does not understand heaven or
true "fame" in the eyes of God. This attitude leads
only to excess and drives Beowulf towards chivalry by
which, when he dies, he hopes to be remembered. The
possible ill consequences of such chivalry are also evident in Beorhtnoth, "hero" of *The Battle of Maldon*. In
allowing the invading Northmen to cross the ford for a
fair fight when they were in fact trapped, Beorhtnoth
"was chivalrous rather than strictly heroic." The most
grievous consequence of his action was that he sacri-
ficed "all the men most dear to him" in his own desire
for glory. The truly heroic situation, says Tolkien,
was that of Beorhtnoth's soldiers. "In their situation
heroism was superb. Their duty was unimpaired by the
error of their master." Consequently, "it is the heroism of obedience and love not of pride or willfulness
that is the most heroic and the most moving."[31]

The Christian distinction between true and false

heroism is thus already at work in *Beowulf* and *The Battle of Maldon,* and certainly in *Paradise Lost* true Christian heroism based on obedience is at odds with mere glory won in deeds of arms. The feats of war in *Paradise Lost,* especially the War in Heaven, are best read as a parody of the futility of epic battles. The true heroism depends not on the acclaim of men, but on the love of God, as Adam must discover. The theme is central also in *The Lord of the Rings,* and it helps to explain why we are closer to Frodo and Sam than to Aragorn. The hobbits are more purely heroic in that there is nothing chivalrous about them, and their heroism of obedience burns brightest because it is often without any hope of yielding renown or good name among men. Aragorn, true, is heroic, but he is chivalrous as well, and his fame is significantly reinforced by the acclaim of men. In total contrast is Sam Gamgee, whose part is least publicly acclaimed of all, but who, in the sense in which we are now using the word, is especially heroic. His unfailing devotion to Frodo is exemplary, and here again Sam is a key link in bringing the meaning of the book to the reader, the everyman who admires great deeds but wonders what his own part might be in important events which seem well enough wrought without him.

The spiritual interpretation of heroism is the most significant Christian modification of the epic tradition and contains in essence the other motifs we have named. Their presence in *The Lord of the Rings* will therefore be indicated more briefly. First, if Tolkien is careful to show his most moving moments of heroism in the context of obedience to transcendent principles, he is also careful to point out that the most binding love derives directly from such obedience. The marriages at the end of the trilogy are clearly possible because the quest has been faithfully completed. Also, among the company, the strongest fellowship develops from a shared dedication to the quest and obedience to directives from higher sources of knowledge. The ensuing fellowship is strong enough to break even the age-old enmities between dwarves and elves, as is shown for instance by the intense loyalty the dwarf Gimli feels to the elf Galadriel. The fellowship breaks only when the bond of obedience is also broken, as it is by Boromir, whose pride and lust for personal power are evidence of false heroism.

The love of Sam for Frodo is the most consistent,
and the most heroic, of all such relationships in the
trilogy, and in it the ancillary theme that love sub-
sumes faith and hope becomes plain. Though Frodo does
not waver in faith until the very last moment at the
Cracks of Doom, he loses hope as he and Sam face the
plain of Gorgoroth: "I am tired, weary, I haven't a hope
left" (III,195). Soon he states, even more defeated: "I
never hoped to get across. I can't see any hope of it
now" (III,201). Finally Frodo's hope dissolves entirely, and he tells Sam: "Lead me! As long as you've got
any hope left. Mine is gone" (III,206). Gradually
Frodo's physical power is affected and Sam carries him
on his back. The story is, at this point, almost allegorical, as Sam's charity sustains his master's hope and
faith. And there is no doubt about the contribution of
Sam's heroic love to the success of the quest.

In the last resort, heroic obedience based on love
of God and one's fellows must also involve faith in
God's Providence, so that events that may appear unde-
served or random can be accepted as part of a greater
design. The wiser a man is, the more deeply he can see
into that design. So Gandalf, for example, knows that
Frodo and Gollum may meet. He also guesses that Aragorn
has used the *palantír,* and his knowledge depends less
on coincidence than on his perception of the design in
events. On the other hand, those characters who are
less wise are more at the mercy of unexplained events.
Merry and Pippin, for example, do not suspect that their
"chance" meeting with the ents is to cause the offensive
that overwhelms Isengard. Early in the story we are
directed to the importance of the complex relations of
chance and Providence by Frodo's question to Tom Bombadil: "Was it just chance that brought you at that moment?" Tom replies, enigmatically: "Just chance brought
me then, if chance you call it. It was no plan of mine,
though I was waiting for you" (I,137). Examples could
be multiplied, but Tolkien plainly enough indicates
throughout *The Lord of the Rings* that on some profound
level a traditional Providence is at work in the unfolding of events. And in a world where men must die, where
there are no havens, where the tragedy of exile is an
enduring truth, the sense, never full, always intermit-
tent, of a providential design, is also a glimpse of
joy.

This essay has been centrally concerned with the analogy between Tolkien and Jung, but it is not simply an "archetypal" assessment of *The Lord of the Rings*. That the trilogy seems to correspond so closely to Jungian classifications certainly redounds to the mutual credit of Tolkien the teller of tales, that he should intuit the structure of the psyche so well, and to Jung the analyst, that he should classify so accurately the elusive images of the poets. For both, man participates in the spiritual traditions of his culture, and in a period such as the present the Christian expression of such a participation must be an especially private and "inner" one. Tolkien, in his theory, is aware of this, and an explication of the trilogy in terms of Jung provides some insights about the structure and dynamics of Tolkien's epic of "interior space." Yet Tolkien believes that his "inner" world partakes of spiritual truth that has found a special embodiment in history: the Word, as Archetype, was made flesh. Consequently, Tolkien insists on the "real" truth of faerie, and his Eucharistic understanding of literature causes him, in *The Lord of the Rings,* to expend great pains on the historical and linguistic background of Middle-earth. We must believe that it is true, and its truth must involve history as well as the great themes deriving, in literature, from the fundamentally important Christian story which is basic as both archetype and history. We find the morality of the story not in doctrinal formulations, which are the staples of allegory, but in the traditional and implicit motifs of Christian heroism, obedience, charity, and providence. Just as, historically, the simmering stock in the cauldron of story is substantially flavored by the Christian ingredient, so are the archetypes in *The Lord of the Rings*.

Notes

1. "On Fairy-Stories," p. 13.   2. Ibid., pp. 14, 68.
3. Lewis, "Psycho-Analysis and Literary Criticism," in *Selected Literary Essays,* ed. Walter Hooper (Cambridge, 1969), pp. 296, 297.   4. Barfield, *Saving the Appearances: A Study in Idolatry* (London, 1957), pp. 133-34.   5. Barfield, *Romanticism Comes of Age* (Middletown, Conn., 1944), pp. 193, 202.

6. Letter to Charles Moorman, 15 May 1959, *Letters of C. S. Lewis,* ed. W. H. Lewis (London, 1966), p. 287.   7. *Beowulf* essay, p. 81.   8. Barfield, *Romanticism,* p. 193.   9. "The Phenomenology of the Spirit in Fairy Tales," in *The Collected Works of C. G. Jung,* ed. Sir Herbert Read, Michael Fordham, Gerhard Adler, trans. R. F. C. Hull, Vol. IX, Pt. I, pp. 231, 233, 235.   10. Ibid., pp. 226, 219; idem, *Mysterium Conjunctionis,* in *Works,* XIV, 325.

11. Jung, "On the Nature of the Psyche," in *Works,* VIII, 203.   12. Jung, "The Spirit in Fairy Tales," in *Works,* Vol. IX, Pt. I, p. 239.   13. Ibid., p. 215.   14. Cf. Jung, "On the Nature of Dreams," in *Works,* VIII, 292; Julands Jacobi, *The Psychology of C. G. Jung* (London, 1962), p. 102; and *Psychology and Alchemy,* in *Works,* XII, 41.   15. Jung, *Aion,* in *Psyche and Symbol,* ed. Violet S. de Laszlo (New York, 1958), p. 6.

16. Jung, "Conscious, Unconscious, and Individuation," in *Works,* Vol. IX, Pt. I, p. 285.   17. Jung, *Memories, Dreams, and Reflections,* trans. Richard and Clara Winston (New York, 1965), p. 392.   18. Jung, "The Psychology of the Child Archetype," in *Works,* Vol. IX, Pt. I, pp. 166, 167.   19. Jung, "On the Nature of Dreams," p. 293.   20. Ibid., p. 227.

21. Jung, *Psychology and Religion: West and East,* in *Works,* XI, 341.   22. See Jung, *Man and His Symbols,* p. 191; Jacobi, *The Psychology of C. G. Jung,* p. 117.   23. Jung, *Aion,* p. 9; *Man and His Symbols,* p. 216.   24. Jung, "Concerning Rebirth," *Works,* Vol. IX, Pt. I, p. 124.   25. Jung, "On the Nature of Dreams," p. 293.

26. Jung, "Concerning Rebirth," pp. 146-47.   27. Jung, "The Spirit in Fairy Tales," pp. 215-17.   28. "On Fairy-Stories," p. 68.   29. Jung, "The Spirit in Fairy Tales," p. 251.   30. *Beowulf* essay, pp. 91-99.

31. *The Homecoming of Beorhtnoth Beorhthelm's Son,* in *The Tolkien Reader,* pp. 21, 22.

David L. Jeffrey

RECOVERY: NAME IN 'THE LORD OF THE RINGS'

Students of Tolkien have often noted that while Tolkien denies allegorical intention in *The Lord of the Rings*,[1] the trilogy does seem to have a few allegorical features. Among these are relatively archetypal items such as Gollum's (Sméagol's) Cainlike murder of his brother Déagol in the story's ur-past, the tree symbolism analogues, the fall of Sauron on March 25 (which Tolkien certainly knew as the date of the Feast of the Annunciation) and also, as I hope to clarify, the name and characterization of Aragorn himself. Typically, these elements have been regarded, in respect of Tolkien's testimony, as part of the writer's richly allusive characterization.

The other notable component of the allusive texture of the trilogy is one Tolkien does not deny: the countless evocations of old Germanic and Gaelic mythology along with traces of their original languages. It has been observed already that the Ring, and Faramir and Éowyn, are to be found in thirteenth-century German literature, that Isildur's story may be read in the *Poetic Edda* and *Nibelungenlied,* and that the speech of the Rohirrim is very close to Old English.[2] (It is actually, in some respects, even closer to Old Norse.) Typically, these elements have also been regarded, in tribute to Tolkien's scholarship, as deliberate attributes of the writer's richly allusive philological style.[3]

It seems to me that both philological allusion and what sometimes appears to be allegory (but which in Tolkien ought to be called, as he calls it, "Recovery") are intrinsic and fundamental expressions of Tolkien's sub-

creative method. Philology and allegory both offer ways
of looking back. Tolkien is, most of us would agree,
heartily interested in looking back, and it is in keeping with this interest that by retrospective and syn-
thetic definition he should offer us access to an understanding of his subcreation's force: "To ask what is the
origin of stories (however qualified)," he says, "is to
ask what is the origin of language and of the mind."[4]
   Again, in contextualizing his "cordial dislike" for
"allegory in all its manifestations," he asserts that he
"much prefer[s] *history*, true or feigned, with its
varied applicability to the thought and experience of
readers."[5] I should like to offer the simple observation that for a medieval philologist the natural conflu-
ence of history, language, and personal thinking comes
at the point of *name*, and that once one has understood
what this means in *The Lord of the Rings*, the appreciation of what formerly appeared to be rich allusion is
likely to be heightened to a new appreciation as the
trilogy's most basic vocabulary.

   In relating the origin of stories to the origin of
language and the mind Tolkien suggests how it is that
"Secondary Belief" must be the arena of a subcreation's
engagement, and thereby doubly demonstrates how fundamental to his art is his acceptance of a traditional
Christian doctrine of Creation. Yet his work resists
Christian allegory. In acknowledging that in traditional one-to-one (text-to-text) terms allegory is not to be
found in *The Lord of the Rings*, R. J. Reilly has offered
a description of the allusive, numinous elements as "inherent morality," and related that to "the sense of a
cosmic moral law" as found in C. S. Lewis and George
Macdonald.[6] One supposes that it is these same numinous
elements that have led enthusiasts to speak of the trilogy as a "personal theology," "like a Bible," or as containing "all the necessary materials for a religion."[7]
The same elements, and fairly enough, lead Patrick Grant
to a sustained Jungian analysis of the archetypal patterns in Tolkien's characters, and to an interpretation
of the trilogy's allusive texture as metaphorical and
mythic in the Jungian sense, rather than, in any received sense, allegorical.[8] These approaches seem to
me to be responding to the right patterns, and I should

like to contribute to an affirmation of their percep-
tions from a philological point of view.

What does Tolkien mean when he avers that he pre-
fers "history" to allegory? Here we need to remember
Tolkien's familiarity with the perspective of medieval
writing, of writing as subcreation. For a medieval
writer, writing is always an analogous activity, a repetition in history of patterns first translated in Creation, and in the Garden of Eden. In the medieval view
all writing that is true will inevitably, even in the
world of fallen fantasy,[9] exemplify. The medieval writer believes that except in primary Creation, and in the
Incarnation, nothing happens for the first time. The
men and events of the Old Testament prefigure those of
the New, and the lives of the Fathers and the saints re-
peat the pattern laid down from the beginning. History
patterns: the medieval view is a view of representative
history, of history *sub specie aeternitatis*. Or history
as poetry.

In quite traditional vocabulary, then, it is possible to see that Tolkien's medievalism makes available
insights into subcreation (and Secondary Belief) parallel to those afforded by the more recent vocabulary of
Jung. I say "parallel," not "coeval," because Tolkien,
like Lewis and Barfield, submits his appreciation of
archetypes to a traditional acknowledgment of creation.
As Patrick Grant puts it, "Lewis's criticism that Jung
offers a myth to explain a myth can be met only by assertion: there is a myth that is true, and fundamental."[10] In everything he writes, but particularly
clearly in *On Fairy-Stories,* a fundamentally true creation is Tolkien's working premise. From out of the
world of fallen fantasy, as he calls it, students (or
writers) gather leaves. But this, though secondary, is
far from invidiously reductive or simply repetitious:

> Who can design a new leaf? The patterns from bud to
> unfolding, and the colours from spring to autumn
> were all discovered by men long ago. But that is
> not true. The seed of the tree can be replanted in
> any soil.... Spring is, of course, not really less
> beautiful because we have seen or heard of other
> like events: like events, never from world's begin-
> ning to world's end the same event. Each leaf, of
> oak and ash and thorn, is a unique embodiment of the

pattern, and for some this very year may be *the* embodiment, the first ever seen and recognized, though
oaks have put forth leaves for countless generations
of men.[11]

Leaf is pattern. Yet since even fallen leaves are not
authorized by men, in the pattern of story the focus is
not on the leaves as allegories but on the art of their
ingathering. Or to put the same thought in another way,
where the medieval writer would say that allegory was
not so much a way of writing as a theory of history (in
which men and events signify, as do words), for Tolkien
the activity he calls "Recovery" (as of leaves) likewise
exemplifies a view of history.

The term "Recovery" presupposes that something has
been lost. The idea, Tolkien tells us, "includes [the]
return and renewal of health,"[12] and here his chthonic
vocabulary reminds us that his doctrines of creation and
subcreation consistently interpret the matrix of art as
"the fantasy of fallen Man."

The Lord of the Rings is a work of art which develops an acute sense of *fall,* the dissipation of the
strength and power of Lothlórien, a Lothlórien largely
recalled in mysterious and powerful utterances of its
ancient tongue. Lothlórien, though diminished, is even
yet a place with a different sense of time (I,243), a
place of *light* and "no stain" (I,365-66), characterized
by a garden, by harmony, and by a mysterious tree (I,
257).

But there came a time, as Glóin puts it, "that a
shadow of disquiet fell upon [his] people" (I,253). The
power of the Dark Lord is shown in estrangement (I,257,
362-63), a separation of men from men, men from elves,
and elves from each other. And we are told that the
elves that fell, fell by "their eagerness for knowledge,
by which Sauron ensnared them" (I,255).[13] We see, too,
that the knowledge by which Sauron ensnares, symbolized
by Orthanc, is very different from the kind of knowledge
desired by the elves when they first made the elf-rings,
not as weapons of war, or conquest. "Those who made
them," Elrond says, "did not desire strength or domination or hoarded wealth, but understanding, making, and
healing, to preserve all things unstained" (I,282). The
elves of old, in a sense, were proto-recoverers. And

Recovery, in every sense in *The Lord of the Rings,* seems
within the pale of belief because the universe is, if
diminished, not totally corrupted. We are shown that
the language of the elves still has the power to "recover" — to still Shelob, the watchers, the Nazgûl. That
is, it is language that most powerfully preserves the
traces, the pattern in the leaf of the world's first
forest. The great opposition in *The Lord of the Rings*
is an opposition between a Recovery of old elven wisdom
and a present obtrusiveness of the knowledge of Orthanc.
It is expressed as a struggle between the language of
elves and the gobble of orcs.

Language makes possible Recovery. For a medieval
philologist there is a rich and multivalent sense in
which language is itself allegory. Or at least the modern philologist recognizes this view of language in the
medieval writers he studies. To express the idea in the
simplest terms, we might say that for a medieval writer
language had central value because it mediates between
mankind's two appreciations of reality: history and
dream. (One could describe the two aspects of medieval
reality in other terms, of course, e.g., time and eternity, nature and grace, memory and desire, etc., and in
the end each would come to mean much the same thing.)
Between history and dream comes language. For a medieval Christian, following Saint Augustine, language provides a paradigm for all human understanding, seeming,
as it does, to express timeless truth through an utter-
ance in time. *Verbum caro factum est* models, in the
Word, the relationship of God to the world. But Christian reality contains both appreciations. It is neither
"the Platonic dream of disembodied logos, an intellectual reality totally divorced from the world, nor an
unintelligible [historical] nightmare irredeemably lost
in the world."[14] In medieval Christian reality, God's
word is eternal, external, from the beginning. History
is a kind of continuous writing of the unfolding of
God's word in time, until, as in the words of Isaiah's
vision, "the heavens shall be folded together as a book"
(34:4).

We see then that the primary book, like the primary
creation, remains under the authorship of God. All literature, for the Middle Ages, forms a present gloss on
an absent text, or, in Dante's words, "shadowy manifes-

tations of the vision of God's Book" (*Paradiso*, I, 22).
Yet shadowy or not, fallen or not, in a logo-centric
perspective, text like language itself lives as a medi-
ator, as a conjoiner of realities, and Tolkien affirms
this medieval view of language emphatically, both in
historical terms and as personal perspective in his *Beowulf* essay.[15] But as a medievalist and a philologist
Tolkien also knew that the very closest and most faithful mediation of language — especially between present
and shadowy past — comes in the Recovery made possible
by the meaning of *names*.

Aragorn is a name compounded from elements that
are highly evocative for a philologist who has studied
European languages of the last millennium. The first
syllable, *ar*, is one of the most pregnant monosyllabic
words in the Old English language, and it is found with
cognate meaning in many other Indo-European languages
(e.g., Gk *arêtê;* OIr *ara;* Goth *áirus;* OSw *êru;* ON *árr,
éru, æru;* OHG *êra*). It is glossed in early texts in
four ways,[16] three of which are correlative: as a
person, as a quality of character, and as a personal
action. When *ar* denotes a person it is glossed as
nuntius, apostolus, angelus minister, as in "þa com
dryhtnes *ar* of heofonum," *Guthlac* 656 ("then came the
messenger of the Lord from heaven"). When it signifies
a quality of character the glosses are *honor, dignitas,
gloria, magnificentia, honestas, reverentia,* as in "sie
him *ar* and onweald in rodera rice" ("may he have glory
and power in the kingdom of heaven"), or in "iôva us
þa *ar*, þe þe Gabriel brohte!" ("reveal to us the glory
which Gabriel brought to you"), or in "bringaõ nu
drihtne wlite and *ar*," Ps. 95:7 ("offer the Lord glory
and honour"). When *ar* indicates a personal action, the
glosses read *gratia, misericordia, beneficium, favor,*
as in "cymeõ him seō *ar* of heofnum," or in "þam þe *ar*
seceõ, frofre þe fader on heofnum."
    While the middle syllable of Aragorn could be
thought of as a kind of possessive infix, much more
likely the last two syllables should be taken together
as *agorn*, alluding to OE *agan* (to possess), and to the
OE verb *agangan* (to pass by unnoticed, but also to
surpass; to travel quickly; to come forth; to come to
pass): "geseah he wunder on wite *agangan*" ("he saw a

miracle come to pass"), *Dan*. 270; "aer his tid *aga*";
"þa *agangen* was tynhund wintra fram..." *Edg*. 10; "Wyrd
ne cuþon,...swa hit *agangen* wearð eorla manegum," *Beowulf*, 1234.

It is in the context of all of these associations,
too, that we begin to acquire a fuller understanding of
the name Arwen, the elven lady whom Aragorn loves and
for whom he works and waits. The second syllable of her
name, *wen*, is related to OE *wyn* ("joy"), yielding therefore "the joy of *ar*." But the form *wen* (as opposed to
wyn in *Éowyn*), though it is related to "joy" — "hearpan
wyn, gomen glēobeames" — also has the meanings "pros-
pect," "conviction," "belief," and "expectation," as in
"Him seo *wen* geleah" (Gen. 49,1446; *Beowulf* 2323). It
is also used in the sense of "faith," "in the fullness
of time," or faith in Providence.

We see then that Aragorn has a name charged with
meaning which, even in its application of character history, is an incarnation of the tale's dream structure.
But we see something more: that the encounter of history
and dream finds in name, if not in plot, an interpene-
tration that must recall the Incarnation, that is indeed
a recollection or "Recovery" of the meaning of that
event. Yet association with biblical language is "acci-
dental," tacit rather than explicit, in that Tolkien has
chosen to anchor his referential language beneath the
conscious structure of other mythic formulations (biblical or Germanic) in the subconsciously meaningful deep
structure of Western language itself. The weightiest
register of Strider's full name lies in the access of
its roots to a language spoken before any of the con-
tending tongues of Middle-earth in which his name still
means, at a time when all language was much closer to
one.

The register of deep meaning in Tolkien's names
helps, I think, to guide us away from a bifocal view of
some events which might otherwise be too lightly construed as allegorical in the traditional sense. Yet
even as we recall these events we can at least appreciate how they might easily evoke interpretations both
allegorical and archetypal: Aragorn comes to the great
battle out of the Paths of the Dead and from the sea
(III,123). He is the exiled king who returns (I,409).
It is suggested by Pippin that he is related to Gandalf

(III,146); he is the elf-man, the one by whom that which was long ago separated and estranged is now joined — he speaks of Elrond as "the eldest of all our race" (III, 139), he takes the elf-name Elessar (ON "one who appears in another manner"), and he marries at last an elven lady who is his perfect complement, and who represents the recovery of a joy which overcomes his eros-longing (*Ar*-wen, "the joy of *ar*").

Appropriately then, as symbol of an old wound healed, he is the king who heals, the "Renewer" (III, 139). He employs, symbolically, the *athelas* (OE "spirit of the King, or God"), breathing on the wounded, creating and restoring their health. As Faramir (ON *fara,* to travel) awakens, he speaks:

> "My lord, you called me. I come. What does the king command?"
> "Walk no more in the shadows, but awake!" said Aragorn. "You are weary. Rest a while, and take food, and be ready when I return."
> "I will, lord," said Faramir. "For who would lie idle when the king has returned?" (III,142)

The reign of Aragorn, and that of his heirs, is to be dominion over all Middle-earth, "unto the ending of the world" (III,246). He ushers in a New Law of mercy (III,247), and a New Age: it is no longer the Third Age of Middle-earth. Symbolically, there is a new tree. And though Aragorn dies, his death is not a cause for despair — in fact his coming is meant to banish despair. His final speech is that which promises the transformation of history in the book: "But let us not be overthrown at the final test, who of old renounced the Shadow and the Ring. In sorrow we must go, but not in despair. Behold! we are not bound for ever to the circles of the world, and beyond them is more than memory. Farewell!" (Appendix A, III,344).

Measured against the backdrop of events, we see even more clearly that Aragorn's name is, philologically speaking, incarnational. Language remembers much, and in the perspective provided by names the quasi-allegorical characterization in parts of *The Lord of the Rings* can be seen, mythologically, archetypally, and philologically, as a pattern of "recovery." Characterization and action become a kind of gloss on the name. Or we

could say that Tolkien's subcreation, in respects both
psychological and philological, constitutes, in a manner
analogous to medieval writing, a present gloss on an
absent text.

This idea could, I think, be extended much further
in the whole work. For example, the sensitive handling
of Éowyn's love (OE *eow*, "thou," *wyn*, "joy") for Aragorn, which he must restrain in favor of Arwen, can be
interpreted through a comparison of the meaning of their
names in relation to his own. This sort of speculation
and etymologizing is a game, to be sure, but just such
a philological entertainment as is consistent with the
language-making of the whole trilogy, and it is natural
to the character of mind demonstrated by this philological and medievalist author at every other turn, from
his lectures on *Beowulf* to his notes on *Sir Gawain and
the Green Knight*.

That Tolkien is trying to achieve much more with the
idea of Recovery than the mere calling up of individual
Indo-European languages is made evident in his selection
of language elements which are still powerfully evocative for our residual collective memories because, in
key names from Aragorn to Legolas to Mordor, the mor-
phology and lexicology is so close to roots that the
names are open to understanding in all the tongues of
Middle-earth. The function of philological recovery, as
of the recovery of history, is here much more than the
surface illusion of being conversant in strange tongues:
it is a participatory inculcation in an ancient depth of
language, of word, and of name still accessible to us
all through the subliminal, often unacknowledged, but
persistent half-conversance which we share — despite
that first dark tower.

Much has been written about Tolkien's eucatastrophe
and anagogy, and I will not indulge myself by adding my
own *peroratio* to those insights.[17] But I do think it
fair to conclude by suggesting that what Tolkien would
have us catch sight of in the "sudden glimpse" of the
good fairy story's eucatastrophe is as much an incarnational reality as his Eucharistic (Christian), historical, and philological terminology implies, and that its
narrative realization, as secondary belief, is the realization in story of a primally powerful Word, one which,

as Word, comprises both aspects of reality — history and dream. "Recovery," as he says, "is a regaining — regaining of a clear view." Since now, in the world of fallen fantasy, we see through a glass darkly, we need, as he says, "to clean our windows" to see "things as we are (or were) meant to see them...as things apart from ourselves."[18] The virtue of incarnational language is that, in it, subject and object reacquire their integrity and are not forever confused. In the making of his subcreation and in the response it evokes, Tolkien invites us to see subcreation in Adam's terms, as *naming*, and yet to see the meaning of name in *The Lord of the Rings* as the very pattern in the leaf, the leaf of the world's first forest as the leaf of the world's first book.

Notes

1. R. J. Reilly, *Romantic Religion: A Study of Barfield, Lewis, Williams, and Tolkien* (Athens, 1971), p. 194.   2. J. S. Ryan, "German Mythology Applied: The Extension of the Ritual Folk-Memory," *Folklore*, 77 (1966), 45-57; John Tinkler, "Old English in Rohan," *T & C*, pp. 164-69.   3. Tinkler (p. 169) states that the relationship between Old English and the language of Rohan provides "an added richness in connotation and allusion," and Ryan (p. 57) comments: "The fusion of elements from various sides, Celtic and the Arthurian preliminaries, Germanic primitive, Scandinavian and Middle High German, is necessary as a bridge between this literary world of Middle Earth and our world, the Age of Men, the Fourth Age."   4. "On Fairy-Stories," p. 17.   5. Foreword to the Ballantine edition of *The Lord of the Rings*, p. xi. An index to the "inner history" of the trilogy has been prepared by Robert Foster, *A Guide to Middle Earth* (New York: Ballantine Books, 1974).
6. Reilly, p. 202.   7. Patricia Spacks, "Ethical Pattern in *The Lord of the Rings*," *Critique*, 3 (1959), 36; see also "Power and Meaning in *The Lord of the Rings*," *T & C*.   8. See Patrick Grant, "Tolkien: Archetype and Word," *Cross Currents*, 1973, pp. 365-79. See pp. 88ff. in this volume.   9. "On Fairy-Stories," p. 23.   10. Grant, p. 375. See p. 99 in this volume.
11. "On Fairy-Stories," p. 56.   12. Ibid., p. 57.
13. Sauron's power to estrange the races of Middle-earth and pervert their desires and aspirations is further seen in the

history of Aragorn's ancestors, the men of Númenor, many of whom were destroyed through the counsel of Sauron (App. A, III,317). Similarly, Éowyn becomes dissatisfied with the royal house of Rohan through the teaching of Wormtongue, Sauron's servant. The dwarves, too, are dispersed by the Dark Lord's power (App. A, III,352ff.), and his influence over them, while limited, is described as inculcating a "lust for gold" and power (App. A, III,358).   14. John Freccero, "Dante's Medusa: Allegory and Autobiography," in *By Things Seen: The Ordering of Experience in Medieval Culture,* a forthcoming collection of essays edited by D. L. Jeffrey and R. A. Peck.   15. *Beowulf* essay, pp. 51–104.

16. Also the OE word for "oar" — cf. Greek *eretmon,* in *Odyssey* XXIII, 275–76.   17. See Dorothy Barber, "The Meaning of *The Lord of the Rings,*" *Mankato State College Studies,* 2 (1967), 38–45.   18. "On Fairy-Stories," p. 57.

Paul Kocher

MIDDLE-EARTH: AN IMAGINARY WORLD?

In 1938 when Tolkien was starting to write *The Lord of the Rings* he also delivered a lecture at the University of Saint Andrews in which he offered his views on the types of world that it is the office of fantasy, including his own epic, to "sub-create," as he calls it. Unlike our primary world of daily fact, fantasy's "Secondary Worlds" of the imagination must possess, he said, not only "internal consistency" but also "strangeness and wonder" arising from their "freedom from the domination of observed fact."[1] If this were all, the secondary worlds of faerie would often be connected only very tenuously with the primary world. But Tolkien knew, none better, that no audience can long feel sympathy or interest for persons or things in which they cannot recognize a good deal of themselves and the world of their everyday experience. He therefore added that a secondary world must be "credible, commanding Secondary Belief." And he manifestly expected that secondary worlds would combine the ordinary with the extraordinary, the fictitious with the actual: *"Faërie* contains many things besides elves and fays, and besides dwarfs, witches, trolls, giants or dragons: it holds the seas, the sun, the moon, the sky; and the earth and all things that are in it: tree and bird, water and stone, wine and bread, and ourselves, mortal men, when we are enchanted."[2]
Tolkien followed his own prescription in composing *The Lord of the Rings,* or perhaps he formulated the prescription to justify what he was already intending to write. In either case the answer to the question posed

by the title of this chapter is "Yes, but —." Yes,
Middle-earth is a place of many marvels. But they are
all carefully fitted into a framework of climate and
geography, familiar skies by night, familiar shrubs and
trees, beasts and birds on earth by day, men and manlike
creatures with societies not too different from our own.
Consequently the reader walks through any Middle-earth
landscape with a security of recognition that woos him
on to believe in everything that happens. Familiar but
not too familiar, strange but not too strange. This is
the master rubric that Tolkien bears always in mind when
inventing the world of his epic. In applying the formula in just the right proportions in the right situations
consists much of his preeminence as a writer of fantasy.

Fundamental to Tolkien's method in *The Lord of the
Rings* is a standard literary pose which he assumes in
the prologue and never thereafter relinquishes even in
the appendixes: that he did not himself invent the subject matter of the epic but is only a modern scholar who
is compiling, editing, and eventually translating copies
of very ancient records of Middle-earth which have come
into his hands, he does not say how. To make this claim
sound plausible he constructs an elaborate family tree
for these records, tracing some back to personal narratives by the four hobbit heroes of the War of the Ring,
others to manuscripts found in libraries at Rivendell
and Minas Tirith, still others to oral tradition (I,
23f.). Then, in order to help give an air of credibility to his account of the War, Tolkien endorses it as
true and calls it history, that is, an authentic narrative of events as they actually happened in the Third
Age. This accolade of history and historical records
he bestows frequently in both prologue and appendixes.
With the Shire Calendar in the year 1601 of the Third
Age, states the prologue, "legend among the Hobbits
first becomes history with a reckoning of years" (I,13).
A few pages farther on, Bilbo's 111th birthday is said
to have occurred in Shire year 1401: "At this point this
History begins" (I,23). And in appendix F Tolkien declares editorially, "The language represented in this
history by English was the *Westron* or 'Common Speech'
of the West-lands of Middle-earth in the Third Age."[3]

Many writers of fantasy would have stopped at this
point. But Tolkien has a constitutional aversion to

leaving Middle-earth afloat too insubstantially in empty
time and place, or perhaps his literary instincts warn
him that it needs a local habitation and a name. Consequently he takes the further crucial step of identifying
it as our own green and solid Earth at some quite remote
epoch in the past. He is able to accomplish this end
most handily in the prologue and appendixes, where he
can sometimes step out of the role of mere editor and
translator into the broader character of commentator on
the peoples and events in the manuscripts he is handling. And he does it usually by comparing conditions
in the Third Age with what they have since become in our
present.

About the hobbits, for instance, the prologue informs the reader that they are "relations of ours,"
closer than elves or dwarves, though the exact nature of
this blood kinship is lost in the mists of time. We and
they have somehow become "estranged" since the Third
Age, and they have dwindled in physical size since then.
Most striking, however, is the news that "those days,
the Third Age of Middle-earth, are now long past, and
the shape of all lands has been changed; but the regions
in which Hobbits then lived were doubtless the same as
those in which they still linger: the North-West of the
Old World, east of the Sea" (I,11).

There is much to digest here. The Middle-earth on
which the hobbits lived is our Earth as it was long ago.
Moreover, they are still here, and though they hide from
us in their silent way, some of us have sometimes seen
them and passed them on under other names into our folklore. Furthermore, the hobbits still live in the region
they call the Shire, which turns out to be "the North-
West of the Old World, east of the Sea." This description can only mean northwestern Europe, however much
changed in topography by eons of wind and wave.

Of course, the maps of Europe in the Third Age drawn
by Tolkien to illustrate his epic show a continent very
different from that of today in its coastline, mountains, rivers, and other major geographical features.
In explanation he points to the forces of erosion, which
wear down mountains, and to advances and recessions of
the sea that have inundated some lands and uncovered
others. Singing of his ancestor Durin, Gimli voices
dwarf tradition of a time when the earth was newly

formed and fair, "the mountains tall" as yet unweath-
ered, and the face of the moon as yet unstained by marks
now visible on it (I,329f.). Gandalf objects to casting
the One Ring into the ocean because "there are many
things in the deep waters; and seas and lands may
change" (I,280). Treebeard can remember his youth when
he wandered over the countries of Tasarinan, Ossiriand,
Neldoreth, and Dorthonion, "And now all those lands lie
under the wave" (II,72). At their parting Galadriel
guesses at some far distant future when "the lands that
lie under the wave are lifted up again" and she and
Treebeard may meet once more on the meadows of Tasarinan
(III,259). Bombadil recalls a distant past, "before the
seas were bent" (I,142). By many such references Tolkien achieves for Middle-earth long perspectives backward and forward in geological time.

One episode in particular, the reign of Morgoth from
his stronghold of Thangorodrim somewhere north of the
Shire for the three thousand years of the First Age,
produces great changes in Middle-earth geography. To
bring about his overthrow the Guardian Valar release
titanic natural forces, which cause the ocean to drown
not only his fortress but a vast area around it, including the elf kingdoms of Beleriand, Nargothrond, Gondo-
lin, Nogrod, and Belagost. Of that stretch of the
northwestern coast only Lindon remains above the waves
to appear on Tolkien's Third Age maps. The flooding of
rebellious Númenor by the One at the end of the Second
Age is a catastrophe of equal magnitude. But Tolkien
gives the realm of Morgoth an extra level of allusive-
ness by describing it as so bitterly cold that after its
destruction "those colds linger still in that region,
though they lie hardly more than a hundred leagues north
of the Shire" (III,321). He goes on to describe the
Forodwaith people living there as "Man of far-off days,"
who have snow houses, like igloos, and sleds and skis
much like those of Eskimos. Add the fact that the
Witch-king of Angmar (hereafter called simply Angmar),
Morgoth's henchman, has powers that wane in summer
and wax in winter and it becomes hard not to associate
Morgoth in some way with a glacial epoch, as various
commentators have already done. In his essay "On
Fairy-Stories" Tolkien refuses to interpret the Norse
god Thórr as a mere personification of thunder.[4] Along

the same lines, it is not his intention, I think, to
portray Morgoth as a personification of an Ice Age.
However, it would seem compatible with his meaning to
consider Morgoth a spirit of evil whose powers have engendered the frozen destructiveness of such an age.
    The possibility thus raised of fixing the three Ages
of Middle-earth in some interglacial lull in the Pleistocene is tempting and may be legitimate, provided that
we do not start looking about for exact data to establish precise chronologies.[5] The data are not there,
and Tolkien has no intention whatever of supplying them.
The art of fantasy flourishes on reticence. To the
question how far in Earth's past the Ages of Middle-
earth lie, Tolkien gives essentially the storyteller's
answer: Once upon a time — and never ask what time.
Choose some interglacial period if you must, he seems to
say, but do not expect me to bind myself by an admission
that you are right. Better for you not to be too sure.
    Tolkien's technique of purposeful ambivalence is
well shown too in the Mûmak of Harad, which Sam sees
fighting on the side of the Southrons against Faramir's
men in Ithilien: "indeed a beast of vast bulk, and the
like of him does not now walk in Middle-earth; his kin
that live still in the latter days are but memories of
his girth and majesty" (II,269). As compared with its
"kin," the elephant of today, the ancestral Mûmak was
far more massive.[6] Is Tolkien hinting that it is a
mammoth? Perhaps, but it is not shaggy, it is coming up
from the warm south, and it is totally unknown to the
hobbits farther north, where that sort of creature might
be expected to abound. Tolkien is equally evasive about
Angmar's huge winged steed, featherless and leathery:
"A creature of an older world maybe it was, whose kind,
lingering in forgotten mountains cold beneath the Moon,
outstayed their day" (II,115). A pterodactyl? It certainly sounds like one, but Tolkien avoids naming it,
and casts all in doubt with a maybe. If it is a pterodactyl, or a close relative, then the Age of Reptiles in
which those species throve is "older" than the Third
Age, apparently much older. Gwaihir is an eagle of
prodigious size whose ancestor "built his eyries in the
inaccessible peaks of the Encircling Mountains when
Middle-earth was young" (III,226). All these half-
mythical creatures of Middle-earth are meant to subsist

partly in our world, partly in another in which the
imagination can make of them what it will.

Tolkien's lifelong interest in astronomy tempts him
into observations which have a bearing on the distance
of Middle-earth back in Earth's prehistory. In appendix
D, opening a discussion of the calendars devised by its
various peoples, he remarks, "The Calendar in the Shire
differed in several features from ours. The year no
doubt was of the same length, for long ago as those
times are now reckoned in years and lives of men, they
were not very remote according to the memory of the
Earth" (III,385). A footnote on the same page gives
"365 days, 5 hours, 48 minutes, 46 seconds" as the period of Earth's annual revolution around the sun according
to our best modern measurements. The year length for
Middle-earth of the Third Age was the same, Tolkien
says. In other words, Earth's orbit around the sun (or
vice versa) was the same then as it is now. This bit of
information is not as informative as it looks. In the
absence of modern technology nobody before today could
possibly have calculated the orbit with sufficient accu-
racy to tell at what epoch it began being different. .
But the implication is that at least the Third Age was
not many millions of years ago. Tolkien wants for Middle-earth distance, not invisibility.

.To strengthen visibility, and also to counterbalance
the alien topography of Middle-earth's Europe, Tolkien
lights its night skies with the planets and constella-
tions we know, however different their names. Orion is
seen by hobbits and elves meeting in the Shire woods:
"There leaned up, as he climbed over the rim of the
world, the Swordsman of the Sky, Menelvagor with his
shining belt" (I,91). Unmistakably Orion. Looking out
the window of the inn at Bree, "Frodo saw that the night
was clear. The Sickle was swinging bright above the
shoulders of Bree-hill" (I,187). Tolkien takes the
trouble to add a footnote on that page, that "the Sickle" is "the Hobbits' name for the Plough or Great Bear."
Glowing like a jewel of fire "Red Borgil" would seem to
be Mars. Eärendil's star is surely Venus, because Bilbo
describes it as shining just after the setting sun ("behind the Sun and light of Moon") and just before the
rising sun ("a distant flame before the Sun,/ a wonder
ere the waking dawn") (I,249).

The heavens of Middle-earth and Earth being not noticeably dissimilar, the lapse of time between the two epochs is short by planetary standards ("the memory of the Earth"), however long it may seem "in years and lives of men." Middle-earth has the same seasons we have in the same length of year, which means that it tilts its northern and southern hemispheres alternately toward and away from the sun as does Earth today. And apparently its days and nights are of the usual duration, which means that Middle-earth rotates on its axis in our twenty-four-hour period. All these are comfortable touches designed not only to show that Middle-earth could not possibly be another planet but also to reassure the reader that fundamentally he is on home territory. I have described the phenomena above in modern heliocentric terms, but they are equally valid for a geocentric view, which there is reason to think the peoples of the Third Age believed in, as will be discussed in a moment.

Strange but not too strange. Further to offset the alienness of the large-scale topography of Third Age Europe, Tolkien makes sure that on the small scale its local terrain, climate, and dominant flora and fauna are much as we know them today. We feel at ease with them at once. Spring in the Shire brings warm sun, a wind from the south, new green "shimmering in the fields" and Sam clipping the grass borders of Frodo's lawn. Tobacco grows in the more sheltered bottomland. The fox that sees the hobbits sleeping out overnight as they leave the Shire sniffs and marvels aloud in intelligent speech, but it is a fox, not a Jabberwock. The travelers are later spied upon by birds but they are crows, ordinary in everything except a heightened consciousness. When the fellowship depart from Lórien they hear "the high distant song of larks" (I,388). Fangorn Forest may be dire and mysterious but its trees are the same oaks, chestnuts, beeches, and rowans that make up our woods. As for the day-by-day scenery and climate through which his travelers move on their many journeys, no writer was ever more constantly aware than Tolkien of all the details of mountain, grassland, wood, and swamp, of variations in temperature, wind or calm, rain or cloud, the quality of sunlight and starlight, the hues of each particular sunset. He keeps our senses wide

awake. Picking out at random almost any one day during
Frodo's tramp to Rivendell or Aragorn's pursuit of the
orcs, a reader is likelier than not to be told exactly
what the weather was and what their camping spot for the
night looked like. Given this unbroken running account
of familiar homely things, he is buoyed by a psychological reassurance that never fails him, and that allows
him to absorb very large doses of the marvelous without
disbelieving it. This is one of the hallmarks of Tolkien's personal style in fantasy.

As summarized in appendixes A and B the formal history of Middle-earth begins with the temptation and fall
of the great elf leader Fëanor in Valinor and extends
for about ten thousand years into the start of the
Fourth Age. But into *The Lord of the Rings* Tolkien in-
troduces the two oldest living beings on earth, Bombadil
and Treebeard, whose memories stretch much farther back,
to the first beginnings of life on the planet. Through
them he is able to give his story full chronological
depth by opening up the longest possible vistas into the
past of its various races. Bombadil lived in unimagin-
able times before there was any vegetation, before even
the rains began to fall. He saw the coming of men, "the
Big People," and hobbits, "the little People." Before
that the elves, earliest of intelligent peoples, passed
him on their way westward from some unknown birthplace
to the continent's edge, and thence across the sea to
Valinor. All this "before the seas were bent" or Morgoth came to Middle-earth from Outside to breed his
loathsome orcs.

For his part, Treebeard also antedated the elves,
but ents did not know how to speak until the first wan-
dering elves taught them. Treebeard has seen the day
when the separate patches of forest surviving into the
Third Age were joined in one unending woodland that covered the face of primeval Europe. And, along with the
other ents, he has suffered the loss of the entwives,
the females of his species, who in some prehistoric time
left the woods to practice agriculture in the open
fields and there taught their arts to primitive men.
This is almost a parable of how Earth's originally no-
madic tribes settled down in one place when they learned
to till the soil.

All these are glimpses into Middle-earth's prehis-

toric past. At the end of his epic Tolkien inserts also
some forebodings of its future which will make Earth
what it is today. Apart from gigantic geological up-
heavals still to come, he shows the initial steps in a
long process of retreat or disappearance by all other
intelligent species, which will leave man effectually
alone on Earth. The greater elves are already going
home to Eldamar, from which they will not return, while
the lesser ones who remain sink into oblivion. Orcs
shut themselves into their caverns under the mountains.
After an estrangement from mankind, as remarked in the
prologue, hobbits will retire from all communication
with us, reduced in size, numbers, and importance. The
slow reproductive rate of the dwarves foreshadows their
gradual extinction, leaving behind them imperishable
monuments of stone. Ents may still be there in our forests, but what forests have we left? The process of ex-
termination is already well under way in the Third Age,
and in works outside the epic Tolkien bitterly deplores
its climax today. The hunger men still feel to converse
with birds and animals is a residual trace of the free
intercourse between the species prevailing on Middle-
earth, and since lost.[7]
     Tolkien is sure that modern man's belief that he is
the only intelligent species on Earth has not been good
for him. Cut off from nature and its multitudes of
living beings, mankind has developed a hard, artificial
industrialism stifling to that side of him which is sympathetic, imaginative, free. One symptom of our loss
is the trivializing in contemporary folklore and fairy
tales of the lordly elves and formidable dwarves traditional to them. In appendix F of his epic Tolkien con-
demns with angry sadness the "fancies either pretty or
silly" (III,415) which now dishonor those and other
great races of Middle-earth. "Smith of Wootton Major,"
written later, is a short story dealing in part with
the scorn of our skeptics for a charming world of fancy
that their imaginations are no longer flexible enough to
enter. According to the essay "On Fairy-Stories," creative fantasy has the power to heal this blindness by
"Recovery" of fresh knowledge of ourselves and the world
about us, and of the kindly insight we once had into
other species, other minds.
     But to return to Middle-earth. One region of it is

so far outside our experience that Tolkien can only ask
us to take it completely on faith. This region contains
the Undying Lands situated far out in the ocean west of
the continental land mass, home of the Guardian Valar
and their pupils, the immortal elves. Eldamar of the
elves is definitely an island, but nearby Valinor seems
to be attached to a "mighty Mountain Wall" encircling
the whole of Middle-earth. Both places are therefore
at World's End, the Uttermost West, beyond which living
beings cannot go. Early in the First Age and before,
access to the Undying Lands was by an arduous though
otherwise ordinary sea voyage, but elves were the only
race permitted to make it. After their rebellion and
self-exile in that age, Elbereth Star-kindler, Queen of
the Valar, cast a deep belt of shadow across its ocean
approaches, through which the exiles could return only
when forgiven, as most of them were after Morgoth's defeat at the end of the age.[8] When this barrier proved
insufficient in the Second Age to keep out the armadas
of Númenor sailing in to seize immortality by force, the
One made the Undying Lands forever inaccessible to men.

Because of the integral place these lands have in
the geography and spiritual history of Middle-earth they
are not strictly an other-world. Their closest counterpart in literature is in those early medieval Celtic
tales known as *imrama,* about voyages made by Irish ex-
plorers to the western Atlantic in search of the Land
of Promise. That Tolkien knew these tales is clear, for
he wrote a poem which he entitled "Imram" narrating such
a voyage by Saint Brendan, which takes him after seven
years of adventure to an island of refuge set aside by
God for his saints. In the Latin prose version of the
Brendan search, almost certainly read and used by Tolkien for his poem,[9] the Land of Promise has many elements in common with the Undying Lands of *The Lord of
the Rings,* raising the possibility that it also provided
Tolkien with ideas for his epic.

For instance, Brendan's Land of Promise is screened
by a miraculous circle of darkness through which all
comers must pass, as the Undying Lands are walled off by
Elbereth's belt of shadow. The saint and his monks are
allowed to walk only to a river where an angel in the
form of a shining man forbids them to advance farther
and sends them back to Ireland. Similarly, the Valar

are demiurgic spirits in human or elfin form, radiant
in appearance, and they not only exile the elves at one
time but also impose the Ban against all mankind which
precipitates so much tragedy in the epic. The angel
tells Brendan that the Land of Promise is being reserved
by God for a refuge at a future time when Christians
will be persecuted. Likewise, the Valar have occupied
the Undying Lands "because of their love and desire for
the Children of God (Erusén) for whom they were to prepare the 'realm'" against the day when elves and men
shall have attained "their future forms."[10] Most important for our present purposes, both lands are at the
extreme western limit of the physical world but still
a geographical part of it.

If the navigable sea has any such boundaries, Middle-earth cannot be a rounded sphere as we now conceive
Earth. In the imrama tales this point posed no difficulty to the wonder-oriented Celtic mind of the Dark
Ages, which popularly accepted the world as bounded and
flat anyway, or, when it did not, was quite willing to
forget roundness under the spell of a good story. But
is such a prescientific cosmology intended by Tolkien
for Middle-earth? He never discusses the question explicitly one way or the other. He leaves us to survey
the text of the epic and its appendixes for ourselves.
Quite possibly he considers the question to be of no
real importance to the story, and so is indifferent
whether it is raised or not. Those who wish to raise it
will find, I think, that none of the astronomical passages are incompatible with a geocentric view of a flat,
saucerlike Middle-earth. Since such a view is implicit
in the conception of Valinor as being at World's End,
consistency would require its acceptance as representing
the beliefs of the inhabitants of Middle-earth.

But does the divine act of the One in removing the
Undying Lands "for ever from the circles of the world"
at the end of the Second Age signal a change to a more
advanced astronomy? Possibly so, if that cryptic phrase
means that they were taken out of the physical continuum
of Middle-earth, which then becomes free to be spherical. One difficulty is that the encircling mountains
may still be there (the text is silent). Also, Tolkien
continues to allow the elves still on Middle-earth during the Third Age to act as if the Undying Lands are

visible and reachable. In the *palantír* at the Grey Havens Gildor and his company still can see Valinor, where
the white figure of Elbereth stands gazing out and lis-
tening to their prayers. And, returning home when the
Fourth Age begins, the great elves have only to take
ships from the Havens, though these have been specially
built by Círdan for the journey, to be sure. On the
whole it seems wise not to inquire too curiously into a
question that Tolkien himself chooses to ignore.

The appendixes are not mere barnacles on the epic as
some critical opinion would have them. For example, appendix D on the calendars of Middle-earth and appendixes
E and F on its languages so orient their specialized
topics as to become facets of the cultural history of
all the major races. By this method the basic traits of
each are revealed. Elvish empathy for the gradations of
growth and dormancy in vegetation is reflected in their
division of the year into six, rather than four, seasons, and these of unequal length. The Númenoreans' in-
sensitivity to such gradations, and preoccupation rather
with practical affairs, lead to their abandonment of
those divisions and substitution of twelve mathematical-
ly equal months. The hobbit love of holidays and feast-
ing multiplies Lithedays in the summer and Yuledays in
the winter, all given over to parties. That the elves
are indeed "People of the Stars" and worshipers of the
Valar could be known, if from no other source, from the
objects and persons determining the names they give to
the six days of their week: Stars, Sun, Moon, the Two
Trees (of Valinor), the Heavens, and the Valar. They
also have many special names for the hours of star-
opening and star-fading. The experience of Númenoreans
exclusively with the White Tree causes them to substitute its name for that of Two Trees and, being great
mariners, they insert a Sea-day after Heavens' Day.
Conservative by nature, the hobbits take over the Númenorean week but soon forget its meaning.

Nothing tells more about a people than the language
it speaks and writes. This is bound to be a product of
its psychological peculiarities, its traditions, its
institutions, its whole outlook on life. Well aware of
this truth, Tolkien as a professional philologist makes
of his appendixes E and F on the languages he has invented for the several races of Middle-earth not only

a tour de force of philological analytic imagination but
also one more revelation of the races themselves from a
new direction. These appendixes have the added interest
of being the adult equivalent of Tolkien's boyhood games
with invented tongues. Aimed first at demonstrating the
alphabets, pronunciation, and to some extent the grammar
of the two inflected, superbly melodious Elvish dia-
lects, Quenya and Sindarin, their material evidently
comes straight out of that "history of Elvish tongues"
which Tolkien prepared in the 1930s before he came to
write *The Lord of the Rings*. When this history proved
unpublishable he set it aside in order to proceed with
a narrative about the races who spoke these languages.
So the epic was born.

Nobody knows better than Tolkien that languages are
not static but change continually. Hence part of the
function of appendix E is to trace some of the develop-
ments of the original Elvish spoken and written speech
into Númenorean, and thence into Westron, the "Common
Speech" of the West. Inevitably, I suppose, the laws
of linguistic evolution which Tolkien sees at work on
Middle-earth are the same as those discovered by modern
philology to have governed the development of the Indo-
European tongues in recent millennia on Earth. In this
way another parallel is drawn, this time in the realm of
philology, between events on ancient Middle-earth and
those known to have taken place among us in our own era.

The linguistic history of Middle-earth corroborates
and fleshes out other aspects of its history, with a
corresponding gain in the credibility of all. In language, as in much else, the Noldor elves who have
crossed the sea to Valinor are the fountainhead of culture. They carry back with them to Middle-earth the
noble Quenya speech and the first written alphabet, invented by their most brilliant genius, Fëanor, who also
made the *Silmarilli*. Cultural contact with the Sindar
elves, who have remained behind on the continent, en-
riches both groups, modifies their speech and writing,
and spreads their influence eastward among the Edain of
the north and the dwarves of Moria to the south. Even
the orcs are affected. When given the island of Númenor, the Edain, too, abandon their former linguistic
patterns in favor of the Elvish. It is a sign of the
arrogance and rebellion to come that gradually they cast

off all things Elvish and revert to a version of their
former tongue. Out of this in later years after their
destruction there emerges in the Gondor lands they have
settled the *lingua franca* of the west known as Westron,
bearing the mark of influences of the more primitive
human tribes already there as well as others from com-
merce with remaining colonies of elves. The rivalry between Westron and Sauron's Black Speech, spoken by all
his servants, typifies the enmity of the two cultures,
if Sauron's tyranny can be called a culture. This bald
summary can give but a paltry idea of the profusion of
detail poured in by Tolkien to show how the languages
of Middle-earth both shape and reflect the destinies of
those who use them.

Already noticed in the foregoing pages are many instances of Tolkien's art in gaining credence for his
history of Middle-earth by introducing episodes of various sorts that tease us with their resemblance to episodes that we know have actually occurred in our not too
distant past. A few more parallels, which designedly
are never quite parallel, deserve mention too because
they skirt the edges of large events in the history of
Western civilization.[11] Just as Earth has seen wave
after wave of tribal migrations into Europe from east
and north, so on Middle-earth the elves, the Edain, the
Rohirrim, and the hobbits have drifted west at various
periods from the same directions. Also, our Europe has
warred from early times against Arabs from the south and
Persians, Mongols, Turks from the Near or Far East.
Similarly Gondor resists Easterlings and Southrons, who
have pressed against its borders for millennia and have
become natural allies of Sauron. The Haradrim of the
south even recall Saracens in their swarthy hue, weapons, and armor, and suggest other non-European armies
in their use of elephant ancestors, while the Wainriders
from the east come in wagons rather like those of the
Tartar hordes. The men of Gondor live and fight in a
kind of legendary Arthurian, proto-medieval mode, and
the Rohirrim differ from early Anglo-Saxons mainly in
living by the horse, like Cossacks.

The Tolkien style in creating secondary worlds
did not spring full-blown but developed out of his experience in writing *The Hobbit,* his first attempt at
narrative. In that story Bilbo travels from Shire to

Rivendell, as Frodo does, and meets Gandalf, Elrond, Gollum, and other characters who appear also in the epic. But the world of *The Hobbit* is not called Middle-earth, its vegetation and creatures are not visualized in patient detail, and it has no larger geographical or historical context whatever. Nor are the characters the same, although they bear the same names. Gandalf is merely a funny old wizard, for instance. And in a mistaken attempt to please an audience of children Tolkien trivializes and ridicules his elves and dwarves in precisely the manner he later comes to deplore. To call *The Lord of the Rings* a sequel to this childhood tale, as Tolkien does for the sake of continuity in the Ring plot, is to disguise the immense progress in technique evident in his epic fantasy.

Having once found his characteristic combination of the familiar with the unfamiliar, Tolkien never departed from it in any of the short verse and prose fiction he wrote after finishing the epic.[12] "The Homecoming of Beorhtnoth" is an imagined sequel to the battle of Maldon between Vikings and Saxons in Essex in A.D.991. "Farmer Giles of Ham" is set in the valley of the Thames in pre-Arthurian Britain. "Smith of Wootton Major" takes place in an essentially medieval English village, slightly hobbitized, which is a point of departure and return for excursions into a country called Faery. "Imram" tells of Saint Brendan's sea voyage into the west in the sixth century. It starts and ends in Ireland. "The Lay of Aotrou and Itroun" is a Breton lay centering on the south coast of Britain in the chivalric age. "Leaf by Niggle" shows us a modern English village complete with neighbors, bicycles, housing regulations, a town council, and the rest, before taking off into a rather minutely pictured landscape where the soul after death goes through purgation.

In his unfinished *The Silmarillion* Tolkien faces the same problem in naturalizing the potentially fabulous happenings of Middle-earth's First Age.

Notes

1. "On Fairy-Stories," p. 47.   2. Ibid., p. 9.   3. III, 405. Cf. similar statements in I, 17; III, 313, 385, and espe-

cially 411.   4. "On Fairy-Stories," pp. 24-25.   5. Ransack-
ing the Pleistocene for niches into which to fit the ages of
Middle-earth is a pleasant pastime, which one hopes the players
of the game are not taking seriously. See Margaret Howes, "The
Elder Ages and the Later Glaciations of the Pleistocene Epoch,"
Tolkien Journal, 4, No. 2 (1967), which picks a span from
95,000 years to 65,000 years ago.
    6. Cf. Sam's bestiary poem entitled "Oliphaunt" in *The Ad-
ventures of Tom Bombadil* (Boston, 1963).   7. "On Fairy-
Stories" considers communication with the animal world a basic
human need. See *Master of Middle-earth*, chap. 5. On the wan-
ton destruction of trees, see the introductory note to "Tree
and Leaf" in *Tolkien Reader*, p. 2, and of course many passages
about the ents in the epic itself.   8. The description I give
of the Valar and their country in this and subsequent para-
graphs is a blending of information from *The Lord of the Rings*
(chiefly appendixes A and B) with elaborations later published
by Tolkien in *The Road Goes Ever On* (Boston, 1967), pp. 65-66.
9. The *Navigatio Sancti Brendani Abbatis* is discussed in detail
in my analysis of Tolkien's "Imram." See *Master of Middle-
earth*, chap. 7.   10. *The Road Goes Ever On*, p. 66.
    11. These examples come mainly from appendixes A and B, but
most of them are alluded to also in the course of the three
volumes of the epic.   12. Detailed readings of each of these
shorter pieces of fiction appear under appropriate headings in
Master of Middle-earth, chap. 7.

Henry B. Parks

TOLKIEN AND THE CRITICAL APPROACH TO STORY

Modern criticism of narrative fiction has long been
worried to distraction by a debate over the relative
ranking of the novel and the romance. Rising as it
largely does out of the eighteenth and nineteenth centuries' intensified version of the ancient argument over
the epistemological status of imaginative literature,
the debate turns on the question of which of the two
genres represents reality more truthfully. Intimidated
in the first place by the prevalence of the positivis-
tic-nominalistic definition of reality, criticism has
tended to place its bets on the novel. Of the two, it
was that genre which could be most readily defended as
according with the imposed notions of reality, truth,
and hence value. Smollett wrote with lofty assurance,
"When the minds of men were debauched, by the imposition
of priestcraft, to the utmost pitch of credulity, the
authors of romance arose." "What a deuce," blustered
Richardson, "do you think I am writing a Romance? Don't
you see that I am copying Nature?"[1] And the judgment
that the novel is superior for its imitation of nature
persists despite changing notions of reality: "It happens that in our present phase of civility, the novel
is the central form of literary art.... [It would always
eschew] the stereotypes which ignore reality, and whose
remoteness from it we identify as absurd.... It cannot
work with...the old laws of the land of romance...,[of]
fantasy, which is a way of deforming reality."[2] Shades
of Peacockiana! Of the romancer this critic believes
"the march of his intellect is like that of a crab,
backward." With Tolkien, one might say, "There is a

sting in this...the sharper for coming from a critic,
who deserves the title of the poet's best friend."[3]

Confronted with this mutiny which arrays the forces
of criticism against itself, romancers and critics of
the romance not surprisingly become doubly intimidated.
If the opposition is correct in maintaining that the
novel owns a kind of privileged access to reality, they
are apparently left alone with the need to defend the
purely imaginative — or, in other words, to perform the
traditional task of speaking for the fictional status of
fiction. But the issue is not always recognized for
what it is, especially when the romance critic is engaged in the close confines of practical criticism.
Here where clear theoretical issues are submerged, he
may allow the opposition's ground of evaluation subtly
to insinuate itself on various levels; he may find himself attempting to redeem a romance by discovering in it
some of those very qualities that point to the novel's
superiority.

Thus Paul Kocher asks "Middle-earth: An Imaginary
World?" thereby beginning a search for the Lost Continent of Mu which splits Tolkien's world into half fictional, half factual and destroys its integrity.[4] I
suspect that Kocher, like those *Beowulf* critics of whom
Tolkien speaks, has been overcome at once by "the glam-
our of Poesis" and by novel-centered criticism. Tolkien's calling the trilogy "history" and referring to
Middle-earth as if it were "our own green and solid
earth" is part of the rhetorical stance proper to establishing the necessary "illusion of history."[5] The element of the ordinary is indeed essential to establishing
credibility, but the ordinary has to do with what is
typical in a story, not with the actual, with history
and geography in themselves. "Northwest of the Old
World, east of the Sea" is equivalent to "East of the
Sun and West of the Moon." The trilogy's "Middle-earth"
is a translation of *Beowulf*'s *middangeard* or "*eormengrund,* the great earth, ringed with *garsecg,* the shoreless sea," part of a cosmology that, as Tolkien says,
"transcends astronomy." And history is transformed in
the "Cauldron of Story" into "Other Time."[6] I think the
answer to Kocher's question *(pax)* is Sidney's question:
"What childe is there, that comming to a Play, and seeing *Thebes* written in great Letters upon an olde doore,
doth believe that it is *Thebes?*"

A similar tendentiousness moves Roger Sale to say that one must distinguish between the wishful Gothic Revivalism of "the artist's" essay "On Fairy-Stories" — a mere personal belief, a nostalgic sentiment that causes Tolkien to blemish the trilogy with ancient themes "known and felt to be old and therefore always a trifle artificial, derived, and decorative" — and the story's central heroic theme, which is "very modern."[7] There is a note of wishfulness and a defensiveness in the intensifying "very." The trilogy is, at its best, a thoroughly modern and realistic representation of the present human condition; if only Tolkien had not trifled with pure artifice: "Frodo among the Nightingales."

Whatever reality story may legitimately be construed to be about, it is first of all "not 'about' anything but itself."[8] And whatever original "matter" a storyteller deals with, once a story begins, the "actual" disappears. In itself this disappearance says nothing about a story's significant relation to "reality," empirical or existential; and though it is well to remember Dante's discovery that "reality" actually stands on its head, that relation is not my principal concern. Tolkien reminds us that "our business with [the story] really only begins when it has been rejected by historians."[9]

Not that Tolkien is immune to the defensiveness that besets the romance critic, nor that his criticism transcends the quarrel I have been discussing. Donald Fry has observed that "he overstates his case" in "*Beowulf: The Monsters and the Critics*,"[10] and Sale has been quick to attack the stance of the essay "On Fairy-Stories." Yet, even though this battle ultimately enervates the critical body, the immediate danger is not a defensiveness and a partiality that is open to view, but rather an unrecognized defensiveness, one unconsciously hidden beneath the guise of the "neutral critic" or the "ideal reader." Such critics as believe themselves finally impartial "are open to every unconscious influence upon their judgement."[11] Much of the value of Tolkien's two essays grows out of the clear partiality which makes for a forceful defense: they provoke us to attend to their subjects, reclaim them for criticism, and, in effect, instigate "a current of true and fresh ideas" not merely about their particular subjects but about narrative fiction as a whole.

To escape the distraction and the debilitating effects of pseudo-arguments over the arrangement of genres
in valuational hierarchies means to renounce notions of
generic touchstones. Tolkien realized that as long as
criticism insisted on superimposing the "epic" upon *Beowulf,* its impression of that work would be distorted.[12]
Matters that are central would seem peripheral; matters
that are peripheral would seem central. Likewise he saw
that devaluations of fairy stories and romances as a
whole were the result of an a priori conviction that
narrative should be, like novels, "realistic" — a bias
that Northrop Frye calls "the representational fallacy."
Thus in the fairy-story essay he attacks those "tran-
scripts of life that receive literary praise" for their
supposed "seriousness." In fact, however, he is attack-
ing by indirection exactly what he attacks directly in
the *Beowulf* essay: not a kind of fiction but a kind of
criticism, one that would describe and judge all stories
in relation to a single type, a "novel-centered" criticism as Frye calls it.[13]

Criticism needs a notion that enables it to recognize that fundamental level where the various narrative
types are equal, a notion about which Tolkien, implicitly and explicitly, teaches us a great deal. Romance is
denigrated because it merely tells a story. "And yet,"
as Frye points out, "if we read *Pride and Prejudice* or
Emma and ask the first question about it which is: what
is Jane Austen doing,...the answer is of course that
she is telling a story."[14] To begin with, novels or
romances are all purely stories. Before criticism can
appreciate the significance of types of stories, then,
it must devise a way of understanding them that does not
finally overlook their nature as stories; it must posit
what I shall call "pure story."

Much of what Frye has written helps us to advance
the notion of "pure story," and what he says about story
coincides in many ways with what Tolkien teaches us.
(Considering the debt that both owe to Kant's proposi-
tion that art expresses "purposefulness without purpose" [*Zweckmässigkeit ohne Zweck*] and to the Romantic-
Symbolist esthetic in general, this is of course not
surprising. After all, Tolkien's Formalist inclinatïons
played a role in that reassessment of *Beowulf* which he
largely initiated.) Like Frye, Tolkien insists that

each story be considered according to the conventions of its own kind; the fairy-story essay is partly an attempt to educate us to romance conventions. More generally, however, Tolkien would have us realize that, as Frye says, "no set of critical standards derived from only one mode can ever assimilate the whole truth about poetry,"[15] or, specifically, that the genres must be understood in their relation to story convention. To this end, Tolkien speaks of the "Secondary World" that the "story-maker" endeavors to create, a notion that has close affinities with Susanne Langer's "virtual world" and is partly intended to express what Frye means by "autonomous verbal structure." When Tolkien says that "the essential face of Faërie is...the Magical — towards Nature," he is expressing a related idea, and he knows it, for elsewhere he points out that all "literary forms" involve "Fantasy" and "Escape."[16]

Tolkien thus urges us toward the realization that all types of stories share a "hypothetical relation," as Frye calls it, to the "Primary World." As a story, a novel no less than a romance achieves an "inner consistency *of reality*" (my italics) or, as Sidney would express it, "doth grow in effect a second nature."[17] A story's "inner consistency" depends always upon a storyteller's abiding by certain conventions — that is, postulates of an essentially unreal nature. The novel may begin, "Robert Cohn was once middleweight boxing champion of Princeton," which is as much as to say, "Once upon a time when pigs spoke rhyme/ And monkeys chewed tobacco."

Tolkien would probably not fully accept that final sentence, or rather what it implies, though Frye would. Frye might say that stories exist for us fundamentally by virtue of convention. Tolkien would demur and say that they exist for us fundamentally by virtue of a storyteller's having made "a Secondary World which your mind can enter"; a story must be granted "imaginative assent" and the "virtual truth" of relating things that "accord with the laws of that world"[18] means something more than, or indeed other than, conforming to conventions — even for those kinds of stories in which conventions are most apparent. Here we have, however, a paradox that must be accounted for.

In the true objectivistic fashion of the Structural-

ist, Frye argues that our comprehending the autonomous
story implies the existence, on an unconscious level, of
a total body of interrelated conventions. That is, the
conventions most readily seen in stories of romance-
inclination point to a latent and continuous archetypal
structure which guarantees sense and which it is criticism's function to make absolutely explicit. Moreover,
since "all fiction is conventionalized"[19] and since
"pure convention"[20] is most frequent in stories of a
traditional bent, it is by way of the study of romance
that criticism articulates this structure. "[In] the
criticism of romance we are led very quickly from what
the individual work says to what the entire convention
it belongs to is saying through the work." Thus also
"[romance] is the structural core of all fiction," the
"kernel of fable."[21] Examination of the corpus of romance reveals the single story of which all others are
variants, the story of the quest of the hero who dies
and is "reborn," the "displaced" version or plausible
analogue of a "central unifying myth," the "pure myth"
in four movements of the dying and reviving god.[22]

For criticism, according to Frye, story must mean
myth or "ultimately *mythos,* a structural organizing
principle." For a completely detached study, that is,
myth represents a verbal structure that is absolutely
autonomous in the sense of being heedless of its own
credibility; it is a "Secondary World" without need of
that artfully realized "illusion of reality." Through
it we come to understand what makes a story a story: the
pure design of an abstract and self-reflexive structure
of meaning. By way of myth, criticism comes to articu-
late the "purely literary world" of total archetypal
form in which stories as stories (and literature as a
whole) exist, the Word or Story informing each story.[23]
This is what "pure story" would mean for Frye; as far
as criticism is concerned, this is the nature of story.

Tolkien would say, "[Here one sees] the inherent
weakness of the analytic (or 'scientific') method:
it finds out much about things that occur in stories,
but little or nothing about their effect in any given
story."[24]

And Frye would reply, "Exactly. Criticism as criticism, properly objective, does not, cannot, speak of the
effect, which is a unique and temporally bound experience."

Tolkien: "Very well. But this means that story itself is totally inaccessible to criticism, that for criticism the gates of Faërie are shut and the keys lost."

Frye: "For criticism, yes. Necessarily. Criticism doesn't address mystery."

Tolkien: "It doesn't unravel mystery, of course, but if it's going to talk about stories, it should address it."

To anyone who has read them, it is clear that Tolkien's essays are much concerned with the need for criticism to preserve a sense of the fullness of story, of story itself. This desire to avoid as far as possible any final violation of "the nature of a story (as a thing told in its entirety)" leads him to admonish those whose critical methods reduce story to a single abstract principle, for taken as a resting place any such principle inevitably distorts one's apprehension of story. "The habit, for instance, of pondering a summarized plot of *Beowulf* [as encouraged by research in comparative folklore, denudes it] of all that gives it particular force or individual life." Folklorists or anthropologists "are inclined to say that any two stories that are built round the same folk-lore motive, or are made up of a generally similar combination of such motives, are 'the same stories.'...[Such statements] are not true in a fairy-story sense, they are not true in art or literature."[25]

Now Frye himself warns against "determinisms in criticism," by which he means the imposition of monolithic frameworks of critical attitudes (Marxist, Freudian, Thomistic, etc.), bodies of thought external to, and hence necessarily alien to, the nature of literature.[26] But Frye does not acknowledge that another kind of deterministic danger is posed by his own monolithic theory of literature. Its principles are supposed to arise from an "inductive survey" of literature itself; but the assumption that criticism as criticism performs only an inductive function leads one to consider each story's essence to be determined by reference to an exhaustive, internal structure, one that is closed and self-generating.[27]

Frye tells us that his proposal for the study of literature as a single order involves "extending the kind of comparative and morphological study now made of

folk tales and ballads into the rest of literature."[28]
Given Tolkien's view of just this kind of study, it is
no accident that the two critics should diverge in their
notions of criticism's overall function. No less than
the Aarne-Krohn method, no less than Vladimir Propp,
Lord Raglan, or Joseph Campbell, no less than the sophisticated Structuralist method of Claude Lévi-Strauss
does Frye begin with an exclusively reductionist move
and end with a One, a principle of necessity that overwhelms the individuality whereby story realizes its
peculiar effect as story. Of course Frye, like Lévi-
Strauss, would allow for variability, but as with Lévi-
Strauss the variable is understood only for its depen-
dence on the one mythic structure. Again, Frye attempts
to avoid a Platonic conception of *mimesis* by positing
mythos as a continuous element reconstructed on the
level of the individual story, each work a monad at once
metaphorically containing and reflecting the total Word.
Nevertheless, we are given to understand that one com-
prehends a story by subconscious reference to the One
"Story," and so Frye arrests criticism within its articulation of a *Monas Monadum*.[29] "[The] individual and
discrete literary experience...melts 'into thin air':
what does not vanish is the total vision which contains
the experience."[30]

Such a defiant leap to the Universal,[31] this arrest
of criticism, Tolkien resists. Unlike Frye, he does not
think such a critical *stasis* inevitable; he would not
have criticism give over an attempt to communicate a
sense of "the colouring, the atmosphere, the unclassifiable individual details,...the general purport that
informs with life the undissected bones of...plot."[32]
Implicitly Tolkien argues that criticism's inevitable
formulation of wholes, of principles of story-necessity,
does not mean that criticism stands finally in its own
"otherness." Its articulation of the typical and the
recurring must not betray story's individuality, the
sense that a story reveals itself uniquely, the sense
of discovered newness that moves the desire to speak of
story in the first place.

Tolkien realizes as well as Frye does that unique-
ness in itself is inapprehensible. Thus at certain
points throughout the fairy-story essay he posits, in
various guises, the notion of a total "Secondary World":

he speaks of the realm of faerie, of the "Cauldron of Story," of the "Tree of Tale," of the "seamless Web of Story." But because he realizes that criticism is in danger when it forgets that it has dealt itself the insoluble problem of the adequate metaphor, he would make us fully conscious of criticism's figurative way of speech. By his shifting of metaphors, he would show us that criticism can never totally secure itself, for it can never exhaust "Secondary World." Each metaphor (and each extension of each) shows criticism inspired by story; each by design conveys a sense of individual story even as it suggests criticism's movement toward a universe of discourse. And because each captures a sense of story itself, each is limited, containing its own principle of corrigibility: faerie is a realm whose "very richness and strangeness tie the tongue"; the "Web of Story" is "seamless," but each story marks a "sharp cut" in its "tapestry"; a "Tree," yes, but trees, "oak and ash and thorn," and every leaf of each "is a unique embodiment of the pattern"; and "if we speak of a Cauldron, we must not wholly forget the Cooks."[33]

A criticism that would be a poetics (and every critical act gestures in this direction) must not allow itself to believe that once it has made story conventions assume the explicit shape of a total Secondary World it has discovered the founding principle of story or has revealed "the secret of the whole" which is a story's virtual world. The critic can only hope, as Tolkien hopes, to "give some glimpses of [his] own imperfect vision" of that whole,[34] for "myth is alive at once and in all its parts, and dies before it can be dissected." Tolkien follows his own advice and frequently speaks of story in parables. He talks of dragons as if they were real: "The dragon wields a physical fire, and covets gold.... [He] is slain with iron in his belly." But he has told us what "real dragons" are; they are dragons "essential both to the machinery and the ideas of a poem or tale."[35] He speaks of elves as if they actually existed: "Our fates are sundered, and our paths seldom meet." And then he immediately moves, adding: "This is true also, even if they are only creations of Man's mind, in 'time' only as reflecting in a particular way one of Man's visions of Truth."[36] One sees criticism oscillating between the story and something other than the story. Tolkien recognizes the difference between a story and talk about a story, but when he speaks story-wise and talks of a Secondary World as if it were alive he does so because that is how story world comes to us — *as if* it were alive.

Thus he is not content to think of "pure story" as a structure of conventions. He would capture story's conventions, but he would capture them in motion, as if in their place. He points toward such a notion as Frye's total form, but is drawn to illuminate the experience realized by its particular embodiment. He would speak from inside the world of story, would express the soul as much as the letter, the illusion that only the conventions animated produce. For Frye it is exactly the illusion that criticism, standing back, cannot deal with. But Tolkien teaches us that criticism can stand back and treat the work as mediately knowable object only when it by turn stands within the experience, the work as immediately known object. Involvement in the presence of the work inspires a desire to bear witness, but witnessing means an evolvement, a going-out and an imitation of presence. Turn and turn about: the critic mediates objectively only insofar as he witnesses faithfully, only when he is conscious of imitating subjectively.

To state the matter differently, criticism is forever a beginning out of the work because the work is a paradoxical "immediate object" (to modify Krieger's term).[37] Even as it exists *about* the story, criticism exists *for* or *toward* the story. (This is another way of expressing Tolkien's clear belief that criticism properly clarifies our way of apprehending story and thus makes us newly receptive to it.) Hence the critic is always partly giving voice to that response that Tolkien calls "Secondary Belief"; he is always partly translating the story in its own tongue. And Tolkien's objection to Coleridge's phrase "willing suspension of disbelief" is grounded in his awareness that insofar as the phrase expresses as a negative (cf. "pseudo-statement") what is a fundamentally positive response, an assent, it implies that criticism is from beginning to end outside the work, is purely antithesis.[38]

A recognition of criticism's beginning out of the work helps us to understand more fully the critical ad-

as easily, assist a reader to clarify his dislike of the
environment in which he is placed. The artist can...be-
come 'subversive' by merely singing in all innocence, of
respite by the Mississippi."[52]

Certainly we may say that as compared with a less
"realistic," a more "realistic" fiction displays a more
strictly defined conception of causality in establishing
its illusions. At the same time the range of probable
possibilities is, in a sense, narrowed and the temporal
compressed into a more immediate linearity. But what
have we here except a more and a less, a continuum of
relatives from whose definition plausible illusion is
nowhere absent? If romancer and realist alike must work
the credible tale, must struggle to make words agree,
the principle of displacement does not serve.

That a more "realistic" fiction figures its design
in a way that can be seen to comport with certain notions of causality does not justify one's saying that
"realism" cloaks design in the guise of representation.
For if one holds a historical point of view consistently, one is compelled to speak of all fiction as "representational," that is, as a function of its intellectual
milieu. But no assumptions about the nature of reality,
even purely supernaturalist or acausal beliefs held
absolutely, release the storyteller from the *task* of
making a story. No more does the performance of one
miracle free a god who desires another of the need to
perform it as well. The critic might speak critically
and say that story guarantees "Story." But this is not
equivalent to saying that one miracle guarantees God,
for God's existence is nowhere dependent, is totally
realized, while "Story's" existence depends everywhere
on stories. One miracle guarantees a possibility — the
possibility of another miracle — not an absolute actuality; one story guarantees the *possibility* of another.
When criticism speaks of "Story" (or total archetypal
form) it is speaking of a *possibility* revealed by its
only actuality, the made story.

Notes

1. Smollett quoted from the "Preface" to *Roderick Random* (1784)
by Miriam Allott, *Novelists on the Novel* (New York, 1959), p.

43; Richardson quoted from the "Letter to Miss Mulso (5 October, 1752)" by Allott, p. 41.   2. Frank Kermode, *The Sense of an Ending* (New York, 1967), pp. 128, 130.   3. *Beowulf* essay, p. 59.   4. Kocher, *Master of Middle-earth* (New York, 1977), pp. 1-17. See pp. 117-32 in this volume.   5. *Beowulf* essay, p. 54. Cf. Susanne Langer's phrase "virtual history."

6. Ibid., p. 67; "On Fairy-Stories," pp. 30-32.   7. Sale, *T & C,* pp. 287, 286.   8. Tolkien, as quoted by Reilly, *T & C,* p. 136.   9. "On Fairy-Stories," p. 30.   10. "Introduction: The Artistry of *Beowulf*" in *The Beowulf Poet,* ed. Fry (Englewood Cliffs, N.J., 1968), p. 1.

11. S. L. Bethell, *Essays on Literary Criticism and the English Tradition* (London, 1948), p. 25.   12. See *Beowulf* essay, esp. pp. 60, 85.   13. Frye, *Anatomy of Criticism* (New York, 1965), p. 132; "On Fairy-Stories," pp. 45, 46; Frye, *Anatomy,* p. 304.   14. Frye, *The Secular Scripture* (Cambridge, 1976), p. 39.   15. Frye, *Anatomy,* p. 62.

16. Ibid., p. 74; "On Fairy-Stories," pp. 28, 43.
17. Frye, *Anatomy,* p. 74. Tolkien's observation that "hypothesis...cannot avoid a gleam of fantasy" ("On Fairy-Stories," p. 66) is not to be missed.   18. "On Fairy-Stories," p. 36. The term "imaginative assent" is from Philip Wheelwright's *The Burning Fountain* (Bloomington, Ind., 1968), pp. 186-206 ("Expressive Statement and Truth").   19. Frye, *Secular Scripture,* p. 45.   20. Frye, *Anatomy,* p. 103.

21. Frye, *Secular Scripture,* pp. 60, 15, 183.   22. See Frye, *Anatomy,* pp. 158ff., 192ff.   23. Ibid., pp. 341, 134-39.   24. "On Fairy-Stories," p. 24 n.1.   25. Ibid., p. 22; *Beowulf* essay, p. 62; "On Fairy-Stories," p. 22.

26. Frye, *Anatomy,* p. 6.   27. Cf. Paul Ricœur, "Structure and Hermeneutics" in *The Conflict of Interpretations,* ed. Don Ihde (Evanston, Ill., 1974), pp. 27-61.   28. Frye, *Anatomy,* p. 104.   29. Cf. Kenneth Burke, "The Encyclopaedic, Two Kinds Of," *Poetry,* 91 (1958), 327.   30. Frye, "Reflections in a Mirror" in *Northrop Frye in Modern Criticism,* ed Murray Krieger (New York, 1966), p. 141.

31. Cf. Murray Krieger, *The Play and Place of Criticism* (Baltimore, 1967), p. 119.   32. "On Fairy-Stories," pp. 22-23.   33. Ibid., pp. 11, 69 n.H, 51, 31.   34. Ibid., p. 16.
35. *Beowulf* essay, pp. 63-64, 74, 59.

36. "On Fairy-Stories," p. 16 and n.1.   37. "Immediate Objectivity" in "The Play and Place of Criticism," title essay of the book (cited), p. 6. I am much indebted to Krieger's insights.   38. "On Fairy-Stories," pp. 36-37.   39. Ibid., p. 44.   40. Frye, *Secular Scripture,* p. 9.

41. Ricœur, *The Symbolism of Evil,* trans. Emerson Buchanan (New York, 1967), p. 24; Don Ihde on Ricœur's thought, "Editor's Introduction" to *The Conflict of Interpretations,* p. xiii.   42. *Beowulf* essay, pp. 56-57, 65, for example.

vantage of a notion of "pure story" which accommodates
the nature of story itself. Once criticism assumes itself to be initially distanced from story's subjective
situation, it renders itself practically incapable of
addressing story on that level of its objective situation which gives rise to illusion. As Tolkien points
out, "Secondary Belief," concomitant to the illusion of
reality, depends on verbal artistry, invention with and
in words. "The achievement of the expression [of the
image], which gives (or seems to give) 'the inner consistency of reality,' is...Art."[39] But a criticism
fixed at a distance cannot deal tellingly with "making"
and the verbal contingency of vital design because it
will ultimately postulate, as Frye shows, a closed
structure which is self-generating, or, in other words,
an isolated principle of necessity.

   "There are," says Frye, "only so many effective ways
of telling a story."[40] Anyone who has read Frye will
acknowledge the sophisticated truth of this statement.
But its sophistication is such that it misses a sophisticated truth of our naïve experience in stories: Tolkien would say that there are as many "effective ways of
telling a story" as there are storytellers who can make
with words that "Sub-Creation" which induces Secondary
Belief. To paraphrase Paul Ricœur on philosophers, the
springing up of storytellers and their works is unfore-
seeable, for "language at its highest level is open."[41]
That is, on the level of the speaker, language is a *new
event*. It is this principle, operating in story by way
of its teller, that assures the difference of each story
and hence the possibility of significant difference,
that is, of the individuality constituting the virtu-
ality of life that marks a story.

   For newness to achieve significance in design, the
storyteller must be gifted — not merely with tradition
and words (common gifts), but in figuring design in
words. That life-in-design which is essential to story
depends, at first, as Tolkien urged in connection with
Beowulf, on what the storyteller does with tradition,[42]
on how he words the Word. "Speak that I may see thee":
when he is successful, the story becomes its own speaker, and we stand in its presence as it offers testimony
about itself, an ethical proof of what it says. One
listens for consistency in proof, but a story's consis-

tency, like that of a personality, is not calculable
as pure necessity. Things "add up," but not after the
fashion of rational numbers and not in ways that can be
anticipated or fully accounted for. This consistency
is accomplished on the level of expression; occurring in
the act of telling, of choosing suitable words and
uniquely suiting word to word, it seems to "happen."
But because Frye treats story purely as structure, he
cannot, as Lévi-Strauss cannot,[43] deal with words,
choice, newness, and suitability and hence cannot speak
to that illusion of life which arises from the inconsis-
tent consistency of story.

Given story's peculiar consistency, it is evident
that the law of necessity informing a Secondary World is
such as is realized through partial recurrence — even as
in the Primary World, "like events [like words], never
from world's beginning to world's end the same event
[the same words]."[44] Story design is never a simplex,
and story necessity is never pure, for recurrence is
never complete. It occurs only and always within a
complex of change where nothing is ever quite itself.
There is no going-back in story, only a going-forward.
Mounting the stairs of Cirith Ungol, Frodo says to
Samwise, "I don't like anything here at all...step or
stone, breath or bone. Earth, air and water all seem
accursed. But so our path is laid." Sam replies, "Yes,
that's so.... [As in] the tales that really mattered, or
the ones that stay in the mind, [folk] seem to have been
just landed in them, usually — their paths were laid
that way, as you put it. But I expect they had lots of
chances, like us, of turning back, only they didn't"
(II,320-21). There is necessity in story, but "folk
seem to have landed" in it; there is necessity, but
characters can talk about it. Necessity occurs in story
as a contingent necessity.

This notion, "contingent necessity," is meant to ac-
commodate the fact that the reality of a Secondary World
depends on our impression that design or necessity appears to gravitate to the words, characters, and events
of a story from ever-changing directions. Considering
"making," one realizes that a storyteller projects some
kind of design, that he moves to his task "controlled"
by a complex of factors such as Coleridge calls the
"initiative."[45] Despite this, he does not have any bet-

velopment within a compressed narrative time scheme; a
circumscribed geography and a significant concern with
the security or danger of specific places in the setting.
    I will discuss these rhetorical devices beginning
with time and space, moving on to the more problematic
point of view and associated stylistic matters, and ending with the complexities of characterization and their
implications.

    The Hobbit covers about a year and emphasizes sea-
sonal change; movements in space are also correlated
with changes in season. Baggins, Thorin, and company
make major changes in position on solstices and equi-
noxes. Simple age-old seasonal associations are con-
ventionally exploited: spring is the time of hopeful
starting out; summer signals the ripening of adventure;
autumn brings despair; winter is total war and death;
spring is peace and joyful return. Generally, in
children's literature, seasons are also specifically
equated with developmental cycles: spring is associated
closely with growth and exploration of the outside
world, winter with a kind of hibernation or growth pla-
teau. Sharing this common pattern are the openings of
The Hobbit and *The Wind in the Willows*. Bilbo and Mole
emerge from their respective holes in the spring of the
year; they return only after much growth and development
have taken place. Their spring beginnings contrast with
the autumn beginning of *The Fellowship of the Ring,*
which heralds another kind of development in Frodo that
leaves him without the impulse ever again to respond to
spring in Middle-earth.
    The three-volume "interlaced" *Lord of the Rings* cov-
ers about one year too, but in *The Hobbit* Tolkien tells
the story straightforwardly and quickly, in digestible
portions, with a feeling of some closure at the end of
each incident. Children, like adults, are capable of
delight in suspense and the unexpected, but they cannot
for long patiently sustain a sense of incompleteness.
Bilbo, in very childlike fashion, having already trav-
eled for months, can hardly stand the short wait (in
days) "on the doorstep"; child readers have barely a
page of waiting before the light beams on the keyhole.
As in this instance, children's literature both divides

and compresses time and, therefore, good children's
books are episodic despite their underlying unity.
    Again in contrast with the trilogy, Tolkien's land-
scape in *The Hobbit* is a circumscribed bifurcated one
with lowlands to the west and forested lands to the east
of the central and longitudinal mountains and river.
This spatial representation quite neatly divides the
world into safe and dangerous sides. Grahame's geography in *The Wind in the Willows* is roughly similar, if
less graphic; there the safe field and rich river cultures oppose the Wild Wood, which lies on the other side
of The River. Such simple geography not only emblemat-
ically indicates outside good and evil but also represents inner states and relative psychic disturbance. So
Mole is threatened and experiences sheer psychological
"Terror of the Wild Wood" just as Bilbo and the dwarves
experience Mirkwood.
    Superficially, Merry's and Pippin's first impression
of Fangorn is similar, but Fangorn is an ambiguous, paradoxical place, unlike most places in children's literature. In children's books, dangerous forests remain
dangerous, unless they are directly tamed through the
characters' development and change. Safe places remain
safe, a source of comfort in tribulation (Toad's home-
sickness in prison is much like Bilbo's on the journey).
Sometimes, however, characters have to fight to regain
their safe places, once they have ventured "across the
river and into the trees." Both Toad, in *The Wind in
the Willows,* and Bilbo have their homes invaded during
their absence and must confront the invaders. Usually
the characters, like Bilbo, have been so strengthened by
their adventures that they are well able to do so. The
trilogy differs in spatial quantity and quality. Places
are more ambiguous; safe places are more seriously
threatened or polluted; they can be cleansed only at
great cost.
    In the matter of maturing adventures underground,
Carroll's *Alice* is the recognized children's literature
exemplum and is, like *The Hobbit,* amenable to both
Freudian and Jungian interpretation.[3] *The Hobbit* is
also much like other children's classics in its depic-
tion of this highly significant space. On the one hand,
no one — certainly not Tolkien — beats Grahame in the
detailed description of what one might call the secure
"domestic underground": comfortable accommodations for

gentlemen of limited (Mole) and extensive (Badger) means.[4] On the other hand, Macdonald shares with Tolkien a fascination with the dangerous "foreign underground": the wonder of mountain caves, their terrors, treasures, and the characteristics of their degenerate inhabitants. The following passage, for instance, is part of Macdonald's long introductory description of the "beautiful terror" of mountains: "But the inside, who shall tell what lies there? Caverns of the awfullest solitude, their walls miles thick, sparkling with ores of gold or silver, copper or iron, tin or mercury, studded perhaps with precious stones — perhaps a brook, with eyeless fish in it, running, running ceaselessly, cold and babbling, through banks crusted with carbuncles and golden topazes, or over a gravel of which some of the stones are rubies and emeralds, perhaps diamonds and sapphires — who can tell?"[5]

As Robert Wolff points out in his study of Macdonald, this passage from *The Princess and Curdie* (1882) and others like it from the totally cave-oriented *The Princess and the Goblin* (1871) closely resemble the writings of the nineteenth-century German Romantics Novalis, Hoffmann, and Tieck.[6] Tolkien's cave descriptions, both in *The Hobbit* and in *The Lord of the Rings,* belong to a long literary line which Macdonald, not Tolkien, introduced into children's literature. Tolkien does, however, combine and relate the safe with the dangerous undergrounds as Grahame and Macdonald do not.

In point of view as in use of time and space Tolkien, in *The Hobbit,* belongs with these writers. The rhetorical element that distinguishes *The Hobbit* most immediately from his later books is the obtrusive narrator. In *The Hobbit,* the narrator is constantly addressing the reader and is thus involved in a kind of "talking to children," as Tolkien himself regretfully points out.[7] This is, indeed, the most usual voice in all the great classics of British children's literature. A rhetorical convention like any other, the obtrusive narrative voice can be used well or badly. When it is well used, the voice can steer the child along the course of a complicated narrative, Socratically raise certain questions in his or her mind, and point to implications beneath the surface of behavior or events. Abused, it can be cloyingly didactic.

In the work of better children's writers, the obtru-

sive narrator is the instrument of emotional sensitivity, moral perception, and playfulness. Lewis Carroll
is working within this convention when he writes:
"'Well!' thought Alice to herself, 'after such a fall
as this, I shall think nothing of tumbling downstairs.
How brave they'll all think me at home! Why I wouldn't
say anything about it even if I fell off the top of the
house.' (Which was very likely true.)"[8] C. S. Lewis,
who readily admits the influence of the rhetoric of
childhood, also uses that convention. He writes, in *The
Lion, the Witch and the Wardrobe,* after the sacrifice of
Aslan: "I hope no one who reads this book has been quite
as miserable as Susan and Lucy were that night; but if
you have been — if you've been up all night and cried
till you have no more tears left in you — you will know
that there comes in the end a sort of quietness. You
feel as if nothing was ever going to happen again."[9]
Tolkien uses it particularly skillfully when he comments
dryly, "You are familiar with Thorin's style on important occasions, so I will not give you any more of it,
though he went on a good deal longer than this" (p.
203), or notes about Bilbo's approach to the dragon's
lair: "Going on from there was the bravest thing he ever
did. The tremendous things that happened afterwards
were as nothing compared to it. He fought the real
battle in the tunnel alone, before he ever saw the vast
danger that lay in wait" (pp. 225f.).
     The continued practice of reading aloud to children
partly accounts for the persistence of the obtrusive
narrator, with its explicitly oral quality. But this
convention has always been more than just mechanical; it
can be a special gift from adult author to child reader.
The obtrusive narrator implicitly promises protection
and companionship even when one is reading alone (or
when childlike characters are left without protectors
like Gandalf). One trusts the voice, at least, to de-
sert neither the characters nor the reader, to say when
one should be afraid and therefore alert and prudent and
when one — either character or reader — can safely ven-
ture on or lay oneself down to sleep. This voice is the
voice of a benevolent anthropomorphic god — not only the
creator but the guardian of the imaginary universe in
which it persuades the reader to dwell.
     Tolkien on occasion used this voice awkwardly, but

naturally turned to it because he was composing a work
directed toward children. When he abandons this voice
in *The Lord of the Rings,* he abandons it for reasons
that really have little to do with theories of what
children feel as readers being so addressed. His particular and growing strengths in "showing" rather than
"telling" work together with esthetic preferences and
theological constructs to change his rhetorical stance.

In "On Fairy-Stories," Tolkien expresses in passing
his dislike for frames and machinery that get between
the reader and the reality of the fantasy.[10] His own
"sub-creation" of the Red Book of Westmarch might have
become such a frame had he elaborated on it more than
half-heartedly or attempted really to keep up the pretense that he was translating Bilbo's or Frodo's words.
His true esthetic preference clearly lies in the omni-
scient, *distant* narrator who comes as little between
the reader and the experience as possible. This "sub-
creator" as Tolkien calls him, seems modeled on Tolkien's Creator — nonanthropomorphic, surveying the world
from afar, more the pure Word than any other manifestation of divinity.[11] "He" is certainly not the obviously
intervening and comforting god, on whom the obtrusive
narrator is modeled.

The obtrusive narrator, whom Tolkien explicitly dis-
liked, is, nevertheless, so ingrained in *The Hobbit* that
to edit him out would deplete the book fatally. Yet
other aspects of Tolkien's style, of which he was less
aware, reveal that the rhetoric of childhood did not
come as naturally or as richly to him as to some of his
predecessors. Particularly noticeable to the reader of
other great children's books is Tolkien's lack of sensory detail. In *The Hobbit,* characters like to eat
but when they get a chance to do so they never seem to
taste or smell their food; it's all dreams of bacon and
eggs. Contrast Tolkien's eating dreams or scenes with
Grahame's evocative prose: "When the girl returned, some
hours later, she carried a tray, with a cup of fragrant
tea steaming on it; and a plate piled up with very hot
buttered toast, cut thick, very brown on both sides,
with butter running through the holes in it in great
golden drops, like honey from the honeycomb. The smell
of that buttered toast simply talked to Toad."[12] The
visually intriguing sport of smoking pipes and blowing

smoke rings is conveyed by Tolkien with far more reality
as an oral satisfaction than is eating. The sense of
touch, exploited by Macdonald and C. S. Lewis after him
is not indulged; sensory discomforts — with which children are unfortunately very familiar — are mentioned but
minimized.

Tolkien thought of himself as having "a very strong
visual imagination" that was "not so strong in other
points." He revealingly doubted "if many authors visu-
alize very closely faces and voices."[13] This suggests
not only that lack of sensory imagination already noted
but also the nature of Tolkien's visual imagination: he
doesn't see things close up very clearly — unlike many
children and writers for children — but has a much longer visual span; he is able to reproduce total landscapes
and see relationships among landmarks; he is basically
uninterested in interior or decorative details. Tolkien
is figuratively farsighted rather than nearsighted.

Tolkien's lack of sensory detail and his long view
are not particularly characteristic of the rhetoric of
childhood, but in other stylistic matters, he is again
among the masters. In *The Hobbit,* there is plenty of
one thing Carroll's Alice wanted: "conversation." Characters talk to each other naturally and with differen-
tiation among their speech patterns. They do not make
speeches much or tell seemingly interminable "digres-
sive" tales, as they are wont to do in the trilogy.
They also make up words, like "bebother" and "confusti-
cation," and use constructions like "miserabler" as
Carroll does. They engage in verbal trickery and combat, riddle games, and raillery — remnants of ancient
verbal pastimes that also appear in Macdonald's and
Carroll's works. Neither of the latter has characters
play the riddle game as straightforwardly as Tolkien
does in the Gollum chapter; however, Macdonald's Curdie
taunts the goblins in much the same way that Bilbo
taunts the spiders in Mirkwood. Another of Macdonald's
characters, Diamond in *At the Back of the North Wind,*
brings back poetry from other worlds and spiritual experiences, inspired in a Caedmonian fashion, as many of
Tolkien's characters are. The general interspersion of
verse and song in the prose narrative is another remnant
of an earlier tradition that has remained longer in
children's fiction than in adult and is exploited by all

of the authors mentioned. Tolkien's most original touch
in the matter of dialogue and the like is to have Gollum
talk the true "rhetoric of children," narcissistic baby
talk; one wonders whether children don't catch on to
this faster than adults.

    The physical and emotional traits of Tolkien's char-
acters and the relationships among them are well within
the rhetoric of childhood. The invention of the beard-
less, three-to-four-foot-tall hobbit is especially so.
In beardlessness and size (roughly the height of the
four-to-seven-year-old child), the hobbit evokes the
most primitive type of identification on the part of
children. Children's literature abounds with characters
from Tom Thumb to Alice whose size is in some fashion
contrasted with the demands of the world around them.
These characters have, in various ways, to use the power
of the psyche to overcome or to take advantage of the
limits of their physical power (which is reflected, on a
deeper level, by the male characters' lack of a beard).
    Significantly, the other notable characteristic of
the hobbits, their hairy feet, is virtually ignored in
the trilogy. These feet symbolize a relationship to the
animal kingdom that often appears in children's literature — where childlike characters are animals, or where
children have special relationships with animals from
whom they receive uncritical affection and toward whom
they can feel superior and grown-up. The hobbits' hairy
feet are, however, a vestigial trait related to much
less conscious identification with animals on the part
of children. Bettelheim, in *The Uses of Enchantment,*
describes a whole cycle of animal transformation stories
as having a repulsion-recognition-integration theme,
through which the child first tries to rid himself of
his "animal" instincts, especially sexuality, then recognizes them as part of himself, and finally integrates
them into his personality and so controls them.[14] The
hobbits' hairy feet are constant reminders of both the
good and bad aspects of one's relationship to animals;
hairy feet are somewhat repulsive but also allow more
freedom of self-expression than even bare feet do. The
child in me is both repelled by the grotesquerie and attracted to the freedom of those hairy feet. After all,
to wear shoes is one of the continuing restraints and
privileges of being grown-up and "civilized."

The hobbit species is truly an original and inspired subcreation. Certain other creatures or features seem less original when one compares, for example, Tolkien's wily chatty dragon with Grahame's "reluctant dragon." And Gollum of *The Hobbit* is preceded by strange, degenerate animal creatures that live in the caves of Macdonald's *The Princess and the Goblin* and *The Princess and Curdie*. The conception of physical and moral degeneration of both species and individuals living away from fresh air and light is also a prominent theme of the two *Princess* books. Macdonald too uses savior birds and in the great battle at the end of *The Princess and Curdie* a battalion of pigeons rescues the outnumbered forces of good.[15]

The character of the hero or heroine is a central issue in the rhetoric of childhood. In contrast to Frodo, Bilbo is the typical hero of children's literature with the typical quest. Bilbo and Frodo are exactly the same age at the beginning of their respective quests, but Bilbo is youthful and inexperienced, Frodo much more mature and relatively learned. In addition, the nature of Frodo's quest is not to find himself but to lose himself and so to find himself on another, other-worldly level. Self-integration of Bilbo's type, not self-transcendence of Frodo's type, is *the* quest of children's literature.

More specifically, Bilbo, like many heroes of children's literature, displays all the outer traits and needs of the period that Freud designates as latency, when Oedipal and sexual conflicts are temporarily at rest. This period corresponds roughly to the elementary-school years. Erikson identifies it as the "fourth age of man" in which the main conflict is one between "industry and inferiority." This is the period when the child must learn the "fundamentals of technology" and become "ready to handle the utensils, the tools, and weapons used by the big people."[16] That is, among other things, what Bilbo is doing: discovering that he has not only inner resources but outer skills — seeing clearly, moving quietly, throwing stones, as well as developing power to wield the sword — that make it possible for him to function in a world less protected than his home.

The break at that particular period of life from home to public school was the most significant trauma

for many an English schoolboy, as we see not only in
adult memoirs but in children's literature of the
schoolboy variety (slang from which sometimes surfaces
in the prose of *The Hobbit*). The struggle to become
one of the boys is present in *The Hobbit* although not so
blatantly as in these realistic novels.

Present too, in the fantasy element of the work, is
the desire to *repress* rather than express competitive
conflict and much of the other psychological conflict of
childhood. This repression is characteristic of another
kind of children's book: Lili Peller, a child psycholo-
gist, calls it "the early tale." The stories that she
so designates have in common a denial of conflicts inherent in the dichotomies of male-female, old-young.
She notes: "In each story we find a group of loyal
friends and we find a Protector who can work magic....
Every member of the group has unique gifts and skills
and foibles.... The magician-Protector stays offstage
or near the wing and the friends' actions and their
feelings really carry the story.... Family relations of
all kinds are nonexistent or they are at the very fringe
of the story.... Most of them [the characters] belong to
different species. Who will compare a monkey with a
toad?"[17] Tolkien's story exhibits many of the repres-
sive elements of "the early tale." One might note especially here the absence of contact with "the opposite
sex," — a trait that *The Hobbit* shares with the major
portion of *The Wind in the Willows*. Without reference
to the clear misogyny of *The Lord of the Rings,* even a
feminist might find Bilbo, as a character in *The Hobbit,*
androgynous rather than misogynous in his bachelorhood.
Either male or female children may, therefore, finally
come to identify with him.[18]

One element of Peller's early tale that Tolkien does
not replicate is a static quality in terms of the growth
and development of the characters. This growth and development in Bilbo is the major theme of the story. But
what Tolkien regarded as the end product of that growth
and development in 1937 is quite different from what he
tried to make it later, by changing the Gollum chapter
after he began the trilogy.[19] In the early version, the
high point of Bilbo's moral development can only be construed as an expanded concept of *justice* that goes beyond selfish desires to acknowledge Bard's claims: "Now

these were fair words and true, if proudly and grimly
spoken; and Bilbo thought that Thorin would at once admit what justice was in them" (p. 275).

Bilbo's subsequent renunciation of the Arkenstone
perhaps foreshadows his later renunciation of the ring
but is well within the morality of fairness and sharing
inculcated in children at an early age. This morality
is synonymous with justice to them; therefore, a child
might be capable of what Bilbo is capable of at the high
point of his moral development in *The Hobbit*.

Mercy, however, is not a concept of childhood, as
many, including Tolkien himself, have been at pains to
point out.[20] Tolkien attempted to write the concept of
mercy into Bilbo's development when he revised *The
Hobbit* in the 1950s. The moment in "Riddles in the
Dark" when Bilbo has a flash of understanding of Gollum's fallen state — "a glimpse of endless unmarked days
without light or hope of betterment, hard stone, cold
fish, sneaking and whispering" (p. 78) — is not part of
the original story nor of the usual rhetoric of childhood.

The "mercy passage" is really connected with the
very unchildlike sacrificial development of Frodo's personality and his acknowledgment of his relationship to
"it," his shadow, Gollum. In *The Lord of the Rings,*
Frodo practically goes mad and the three small creatures
— Frodo, Gollum, and Sam — who move across the devastated landscape are emblematic not only of man's state
in general, but also of the struggle in the divided
psyche among superego, id, and ego.[21] Sam, the ego figure, survives, but he is not, after all, prominent even
among the several "heroes" of the narrative.[22]

Bilbo's resourcefulness and basic sanity are honored
in *The Hobbit,* not overshadowed by saintliness, as Sam's
similar qualities are in the trilogy. The contrast between Bilbo and Frodo as heroes recalls Chesterton's
distinction: "In the fairy tales, the cosmos goes mad,
but the hero does not go mad. In the modern novels, the
hero is mad before the book begins and suffers from the
harsh steadiness and cruel sanity of the cosmos."[23] In
most good children's literature, as in fairy tale, the
hero or heroine appears to represent the healthy developing ego with its capacity for just action and for
survival in *this* world. Bilbo lives. And Bilbo joins

Alice, Curdie, Mole, Rat, and Toad in the gallery of
such sane and down-to-earth protagonists. In this way,
as in others, *The Hobbit* belongs to the great tradition
of "the rhetoric of childhood."

Notes

1. In an early foreword to *The Fellowship of the Ring,* Tolkien
seems to concede that *The Hobbit* was composed for his children:
"Since my children and others of their age, who first heard of
the Ring, have grown older with the years, this book speaks
more plainly of the darker things which lurked only on the borders of the earlier tale" (New York: Ace Books, n.d.), p. 9.
In a late interview with Philip Norman, Tolkien denies that *The
Hobbit* is a children's book and repudiates "anything that in
any way was marked out in 'The Hobbit' as for children instead
of just for people." "The Prevalence of Hobbits," *New York
Times Magazine,* Jan. 15, 1967, p. 100.
    This is in clear contrast to C. S. Lewis who chose the
children's story because it was "the best art-form" for those
things he had to say. Lewis, "Three Ways of Writing for Chil-
dren," in *Of Other Worlds, Essays and Stories,* ed. Walter
Hooper (New York, 1966), p. 23.
    2. Wayne Booth, *The Rhetoric of Fiction* (Chicago, 1961).
3. The most famous of these analyses of Alice is William Emp-
son's "The Child as Swain" in *Some Versions of Pastoral* (New
York, 1950). Randel Helms does the same for *The Hobbit* in "The
Hobbit as Swain," *Tolkien's World* (Boston, 1974), pp. 41-55.
See also Dorothy Matthews, "The Psychological Journey of Bilbo
Baggins" in *A Tolkien Compass,* ed. Jared Lobdell (La Salle,
Ill., 1975), pp. 29-42 and Marion Zimmer Bradley, "Men, Halflings and Hero-Worship," in *T & C,* pp. 109-27.   4. We are introduced to Badger's home thus: "He shuffled on in front of
them, carrying the light and they followed him, nudging each
other in an anticipating sort of way, down a long, gloomy, and,
to tell the truth, decidedly shabby passage, into a sort of
central-hall, out of which they could dimly see other long
tunnel-like passages mysterious and without apparent end. But
there were doors in the hall as well — stout oaken comfortable
looking doors. One of these Badger flung open, and at once
they found themselves in all the glow and warmth of a large
fire-lit kitchen." Another paragraph is devoted to describing
that kitchen, ending with: "The ruddy brick floor smiled up at
the smoky ceiling; the oaken settles, shiny with long wear, ex-
changed cheerful glances with each other; plates on the dresser
grinned at pots on the shelf, and the merry firelight flickered

and played over everything without distinction." Kenneth
Grahame, *The Wind in the Willows* (1908; rpt. New York, 1969,
pp. 58-59.   5. Macdonald, *The Princess and Curdie* (1882; rpt.
London, 1964), p. 11.   Sharing my sense of Tolkien's debt to
Macdonald in this and other ways are both Hugh Crago and Robert
L. Wolff. See Crago, "Remarks on the Nature and Development of
Fantasy," in J. S. Ryan, *Tolkien: Cult or Culture?* (Armidale,
Australia, 1969), Appendix D, esp. pp. 216-20, and Wolff, *The
Golden Key: A Study of the Fiction of George MacDonald* (New
Haven, Conn., 1961), p. 9.
     6. Wolff, pp. 170-71.   7. Tolkien says, "'The Hobbit' was
written in what I should now regard as bad style, as if one
were talking to children." Norman, p. 100.   8. Carroll,
Alice's Adventures in Wonderland (1865; rpt. Baltimore, Md.,
1946), p. 25.   9. Lewis, *The Lion, the Witch and the Wardrobe*
(New York, 1950), p. 128.   10. "On Fairy-Stories," p. 14.
     11. Tolkien in "On Fairy-Stories" uses the word "sub-
creation" and "sub-creator" to describe the writer and his job.
"Sub-creation" seems to designate much the same thing as my extended use of "rhetoric," but refers only to the creation of
fantasy worlds. See p. 37 and passim.   12. Grahame, p. 135.
13. Norman, p. 102.   14. Bettelheim, *The Uses of Enchantment:
The Meaning and Importance of Fairy Tales* (1975; rpt. New York,
1977), pp. 227-310 and passim.   15. Tolkien's very use of the
word "goblin" in *The Hobbit,* which he changes to "orc" in the
trilogy (and in his revision of the Gollum chapter) perhaps
subconsciously reflects his debt to Macdonald.
     16. Erik H. Erikson, "The Eight Ages of Man," *Childhood and
Society,* 2nd ed. (New York, 1963), pp. 247-74, esp. 258-60.
Bilbo also at first resembles the third son or "Dummy" in fairy
tales that Bettelheim analyzes, p. 75.   17. Peller, "Daydreams and Children's Favorite Books," in *The Causes of Behavior,* 2nd ed., ed. Judy F. Rosenblith and Wesley Allinsmith
(Boston, 1970), pp. 469-75.   18. Bettelheim claims that for
children the sex of the protagonist comes not to matter, p. 59.
19. For an analysis of the changes Tolkien made in *The Hobbit*
see Bonniejean Christensen, "Gollum's Character Transformation
in *The Hobbit,*" *Tolkien Compass,* ed. Lobdell, pp. 9-28.
20. Tolkien, "On Fairy-Stories," p. 44. See also Bettelheim,
p. 144.
     21. Compare Tolkien's portrayal of the Frodo-Gollum-Sam
struggles with Freud's description of the close relationship
between the Superego and the Id and of the Ego's struggles to
serve, mediate, and temper both their excesses while developing
and strengthening itself in relation to the outside world. See
Sigmund Freud, *The Ego and the Id,* trans. Joan Rivière (New
York, 1960).   22. Merry and Pippin come closest to being
children's heroes.   23. G. K. Chesterton, "The Dragon's
Grandmother," *Tremendous Truths* (New York, 1927), p. 126.

Joseph McLellan

FRODO AND THE COSMOS: REFLECTIONS ON 'THE SILMARILLION'

The sequel to *The Lord of the Rings* is actually its
prologue, both in narrative time and in the mind of the
creator. Spanning vast landscapes and thousands of
years, the stories in this book tell us what happened in
Tolkien's universe from the beginning of time until that
eventful period, late in the Third Age of the world,
when Frodo Baggins obtained the fateful Ring and (with
a little help from his friends) finally carried it
through numerous perils to its destruction in the Crack
of Doom.

From the viewpoint of the Ring trilogy, what we have
in this new volume is a substantial part (one hopes that
more can be edited and published from the remaining Tolkien manuscripts) of the *Translations from the Elvish* to
which Bilbo Baggins devoted himself for long years after
celebrating his eleventy-first birthday and slipping
quietly out of hobbit society. Its central and longest
part, from which the entire volume takes its name, is
the epic tale of the theft and quest of the silmarils,
three jewels of extraordinary powers which were made by
the hot-tempered elven prince and craftsman Fëanor and
were stolen by Morgoth, a demigod devoted to darkness
and chaos, who wished to make himself master of all
Middle-earth.

The slow unfolding of this story covers centuries
and all sections of the old creation before the earth
was changed (one of the things that happen in the various wars chronicled here is that it becomes round).
Titanic forces struggle after building up their strength
for centuries to prepare for a gigantic encounter. The

central myth, of earthlings banded together under a rash
oath to do hopeless battle against a demigod, is one of
great power and considerable nobility, with splendidly
varied episodes of idyllic love and unearthly joy, wan-
ton destruction and high heroism.

Vast landscapes and towering strongholds are evoked,
only to perish in smoke or tidal waves; twisted creatures — orcs and balrogs and firedrakes — lurch blood-
maddened through the flames; crabbed dwarves plot small-
minded revenge for fancied hurts, and the whole cen-
turies-long, panoramic action works out in massive and
intricate variations a single, simple theme: "Love not
too well the work of thy hands and the devices of thy
heart."

The Silmarillion is the chief book of the collection, but only one; the volume opens with a creation
myth of singular beauty, and continues with a rather
scholarly discussion of the varied demigods who are
known as "the Valar, the Powers of the World." After
the *Silmarillion* proper comes the *Akallabeth,* the history of an island (one word hints that it might be At-
lantis), where human society rose to a level never seen
before or since, and then, through the subtle machina-
tions of Sauron, Morgoth's chief assistant and succes-
sor, provoked its own destruction. Finally comes a
brief historical treatise, *Of the Rings of Power and
the Third Age,* ending with a terse summary of what is
treated so lavishly in *The Lord of the Rings,* mentioning
Frodo once and putting him in cosmic context.

To devotees of the more familiar Tolkien (though not
so much to those superfans who pore over the appendixes)
all of this may come as a bit of a shock. *The Lord of
the Rings* is a special kind of fiction, midway between
medieval romance and modern novel; *The Silmarillion* and
those works which accompany it in this volume are altogether a different kind of writing — primitive in some
places, rather dry and scholarly in others, primarily
epic in style and vision, dealing with the fate of whole
peoples and focusing only momentarily on an occasional
key individual. If the Ring trilogy competes for attention mainly with almost-forgotten medieval romances, *The
Silmarillion* demands comparison with Hesiod and *The
Iliad, Paradise Lost* and Genesis. And although it is
unevenly written (the author would surely have revised

it before publication had he lived), its best parts
stand up well under such comparisons.

What happened to Tolkien's style between *The Silmarillion* and *The Lord of the Rings* is told, or at least
broadly hinted, in his foreword to *The Lord of the
Rings*. After *The Hobbit* was written but before it was
published, he says, he began to work on the Ring trilogy.

> But I did not go on with this sequel, for I wished
> first to complete and set in order the mythology and
> legends of the Elder Days, which had then been tak-
> ing shape for some years. I desired to do this for
> my own satisfaction, and I held little hope that
> other people would be interested in this work, espe-
> cially since it was primarily linguistic in inspira-
> tion and was begun in order to provide the necessary
> background of "history" for Elvish tongues.
> When those whose advice and opinion I sought
> corrected *little hope* to *no hope,* I went back to the
> sequel, encouraged by requests from readers for more
> information concerning hobbits and their adventures.
> But the story was drawn irresistibly towards the
> older world, and became an account of its end and
> passing away before its beginning and middle had
> been told. (I,5)

In other words, Tolkien found an enthusiastic audience for one small corner of his massive vision and no
market at all for the greater part of his imaginings.
And like a true professional (and a hobbit-fancier himself), he adapted — shrank — his vision to suit the
available market. One is reminded of Shakespeare, whose
magnificent series of historical plays produced, offhand
and almost by accident, a minor character named Fal-
staff.

The vision of the First and Second Ages was already
fully formed (it had been accumulating in notebooks
since 1917, twenty years before *The Hobbit* was published), and although he could not publish it as such —
never, in fact, put it into final, publishable form —
Tolkien continued to tinker with its details through the
rest of his life and crammed much of it into the various
appendixes to *The Lord of the Rings*. So the contents of
this posthumous volume will not come as a complete sur-

prise to Tolkien-lovers, though its tone, content, and style have only a tenuous connection with his more familiar work. The task of excerpting a publishable book from the various fragments left by Tolkien was entrusted to his son, Christopher, who explains his lengthy, complex role in a brief, unassuming foreword.

As to its importance in the Tolkien canon, even those (misguided, I believe) who prefer the hobbit books to this newly published material must recognize that the myths of the Elder Days are what make their favorite author unique. These early fantasy writings (though they appear belatedly, four years after his death and six decades after the stories were conceived) are fundamental Tolkien, the underpinning without which he would not have been able to produce his later works in the form that we know. For though the matter of the Ring trilogy is peripheral to what is given here — almost an afterthought — the matter of *The Silmarillion* pervades Tolkien's other fantasies and gives them a flavor unique in that field of writing.

Looked at objectively, Tolkien is not, in fact, a great writer of pure adventure; others are his equal or better at conveying the concrete detail, the breathless excitement of steel clashing with steel, muscles straining in combat, dangers encountered and overcome. And yet his books are literature while theirs are pastimes, entertainment, something to be read quickly and thrown away. The reason, or at least part of it, is that other writers convey adventure and little else (and after a while, one sword cleaving a helmet begins to look like all the others), while Tolkien's stories take place against a background of measureless depth. Frodo moves in a landscape where others have moved before him through long, busy millennia; he comes at the end of a process that began before the sun and moon were sent aloft; he is a part, small but essential, in a timeless war between the forces of order and disorder, and whether he understands it or not — whether the reader understands it or not — that background is ever-present in the creator's mind and it gives Frodo and company a three-dimensional reality that is seldom found in this kind of writing.

Compared to this historic depth, and the thematic and philosophical unity which it underlies, the other

distinctions of the Ring trilogy are relatively insig-
nificant — the richness and variety of invented languages, the intricate geography of Middle-earth, the
array of creatures familiar and exotic that enliven
its landscapes — though these alone would make Tolkien
unique.

In a commercial sense, those who declined to publish
this part of his work in the thirties were surely correct. Our time has not been hospitable to cosmogonies
and epics unless they are cleverly disguised as something else. Even today, it is hard to imagine that this
work would be accepted by a major publisher if there
were any other name on the title page. For that matter,
can you imagine *Hamlet* being welcomed by a modern publisher if it were brought in by an unknown author in
anything like its present form? (One can hear the agent
on the phone: "Bill, they wonder if you could beef up
the Ophelia part a bit. Maybe a nude bathing scene to
prepare for that drowning.")

Artistically, we have been deprived by the forces
that postponed publication of *The Silmarillion* until
now and decreed that it would be a posthumous work with
no final revisions by the author. What we have is imperfect but magnificent in its best moments. Until
this volume appeared, I had felt that Tolkien's greatest service to English letters was his translation of
Sir Gawain and the Green Knight. He has surpassed that
work, and that is no small achievement.

Robert M. Adams

THE HOBBIT HABIT

Readers who have already been involved with hobbitry, Middle-earth, and the fantastic adventure-romances of J. R. R. Tolkien will doubtless recall from the four volumes previously published passing allusions to epic cycles antedating those tales of the Third Age in which Bilbo Baggins and Frodo his faithful nephew play such impressive parts. These hobbit-adventures, which fully occupy not only *The Hobbit* but the three volumes grouped under the generic title *The Lord of the Rings,* describe just two brief moments in the history of Middle-earth, the years 2941-2942 and 3018-3019. Around these concentrations of episode, crucial though they are, lie enormous blank spaces of Middle-earth history; and it was only to be expected that these blanks should have been filled somehow, with legend, myth, genealogy, history, natural history — the busy business of Middle-earth.

So indeed they were; but the filling-in material was never published until now, and now only (it would seem) in part, and subject to considerable editorial arrangement and selection. The actual composition of the Tolkien cycle is thus revealed as *The Hobbit* first, with the mythical backgrounds filled in next, their presence now explaining to some extent that considerable difference of tone and feeling which is noted in the final compositions of the series, *The Lord of the Rings* trilogy. What is published now as *The Silmarillion* is what Tolkien referred to, in the foreword to the trilogy, as "the mythology and legends of the Elder Days" (I,5). He described it there as "work done for my own satisfaction" (I,5) in which he had little hope that other people would be interested. Consultation with friends, he says, changed "*little hope* to *no hope*" (I,5), and so the material remained unpublished.

It appears now, when the first four volumes have established a Tolkien cult; and by that cult the book is now being carried forward to enormous sales. But it is beyond question that there will be far more purchasers of the new volume than will ever read it through, and one suspects that had it been published earlier, it might well have laid a blight on the entire series. For *The Silmarillion*, despite the cuts that have evidently been made in the original materials, the selection and arrangement that have been imposed on them, remains an empty and pompous bore. There are epic elements in it, but they have been smothered by an overgrowth of genealogy.

The narrative is not in itself very sturdy. Oaths, feuds, sword fights, lost cities, doomed lovers, and ill-starred friendships abound; but there is a dearth of characters and an oversupply of stereotypes. The familiar Tolkien division prevails between level-eyed, steely-but-gentle good guys, and snarling, black-minded bad guys; but the action remains exterior and mechanical. Above all, Tolkien has a fascination with names for their own sake that will probably seem excessive to anyone whose favorite light reading is not the first book of Chronicles.

> It came to pass during the second age of the captivity of Melkor that Dwarves came over the Blue Mountains of Ered Luin into Beleriand. Themselves they named Khazâd, but the Sindar called them Naugrim, the Stunted People, and Gonnhirrim, Masters of Stone. Far to the east were the most ancient dwellings of the Naugrim, but they had delved for themselves great halls and mansions, after the manner of their kind, in the eastern side of Ered Luin; and those cities were named in their own tongue Gabilgathol and Tumunzahar. To the north of the great height of Mount Dolmed was Gabilgathol, which the Elves interpreted in their tongue Belegost, that is Mickleburg; and southward was delved Tumunzahar, by the Elves named Nogrod, the Hollowbold. Greatest of all the mansions of the Dwarves was Khazad-dûm, the Dwarrowdelf, Hadhodrond in the Elvish tongue, that

was afterwards in the days of its darkness called
Moria; but it was far off in the Mountains of Mist
beyond the wide leagues of Eriador, and to the Eldar
came but as a name and a rumour from the words of
the Dwarves of the Blue Mountains. (p. 91)

Three or four names for each city of the dwarves
represent only a very small beginning; there is also an
intricate genealogy of elves to be mastered, a complete
pantheon of Valar, various groups and combinations of
men, plus a whole spectrum of special creatures — Un-
goliant, Carcharoth, sundry balrogs, Glaurung, Maiar,
and Periannath, the latter being, as it happens, hobbits.

Such a barricade of grotesque and semipronounceable
names is no small obstacle to a venturesome reader; but
in fact the names are also a good part of the book's
reward. Like the portmanteau words of "Jabberwocky" or
the deeper and more violent conglomerates of *Finnegans
Wake,* many of them sink into the mind, disintegrating
the smooth and accepted conventions of everyday English
to memorable effect. The dragon Smaug, the wicked and
menacing Nazgûl, the ents of Fangorn — such rich and
mouthy names keep the mind busy tangling and untangling
their phonemes. But when one has to keep Elendë (which
is a name of Eldamar) distinct from Elendil the son of
Amandil, and both distinct from Elendur the son of Isildur, while Elrond, Elros, Eluréd, and Elurin hover in
the neighborhood, the effect is an irritating blur.

Such plot as the new book has deals, like the plots
of the previous books, with the recovery of a treasure,
the three precious stones known as the Silmarils. They
were made by Fëanor and filled with the light of the two
trees of Valinor, which makes them very precious indeed.
Stolen by Morgoth or Melkor or Bauglir or Belegurth, the
Dark Lord or the Enemy, they are long sought after and
bitterly quarreled over by various factions and families
among the Noldor. But like others in Tolkien's thesau-
rus of magic and precious stones, they bring to their
possessors more sorrow than satisfaction, so that nobody
really achieves them. One ultimately disappears into
the western heavens, and the two others are thrown away
by their once-ardent pursuers, one into the depths of
the sea, the other into the depths of the earth.

Gollum or Sméagol, from whom Bilbo took the Ring, is by
no means forgotten; but he is shown to be only a tool in
the vast plots of Sauron who is in turn only one of the
agents and lieutenants of Morgoth, the black power of
Mordor, who is the taproot of all evil, and has (it appears) power only as long as the Ring survives.

In truth, the hobbits, Bilbo, Frodo, and their play-
mates, are not altogether equal to the suddenly enlarged
stage onto which they have been thrust. And the actions
they are called on to perform, however elaborately explained, don't really make much practical sense. Frodo,
who has inherited the all-important Ring, is given the
task, not of using it, nor even of concealing it or
throwing it away (as the Silmarils, for example, had
previously been removed very effectively from circula-
tion), but of destroying it in the most dangerous and
impractical of all possible ways — by carrying it un-
aided into the heart of Mordor and casting it into a
volcano. In the various wars preceding and accompanying
this action, the hobbits are dauntless enough, and occasions are provided for them to appear modestly useful;
but essentially their roles are the subordinate ones
assigned in traditional adventure stories to high-
spirited and venturesome boys.

Very likely this circumstance contributes to the
popularity of the hobbit books; readers can enjoy the
spectacle of grandiose actions, but from the point of
view of modest little onlookers — the formula is at
least as old as the alliance of Don Quixote and Sancho
Panza, and it plays off to a gratifying twist when the
unheroic partner unexpectedly pulls off a climactic
feat. In addition, the English specialize in grumpy,
stouthearted, "natural" little people, domestic in their
instincts, but brave as lions when aroused — Mr. Mole
and Mr. Badger of *The Wind in the Willows* come immediately to mind. The hobbits make much the same appeal,
to which Americans are far from immune. Speech patterns
within the books are interestingly assigned. The hobbits speak unceremonious, colloquial, modern English, as
against the antique Malory-cum-King-James-Bible jargon
of the lordly classes. They are free-spoken, natural.
Sam, Frodo's faithful retainer, is a forelock-tugging,
homely countryman with the inevitable bad grammar and
acute simplicity of the type; while the wicked orcs,

brought up amid Mordor's satanic mills, gargle a debased
cockney, complete with Ow and Garn.

Middle-earth is very British, in fact, physically as
well as socially. Not the least of Tolkien's charms is
his gift for describing a rural landscape in loving,
close detail. The hobbits are useful here in giving human dimensions and sensations to the story; they relish
the landscapes and the homely physical pleasures to be
found amid them. They love to eat, drink beer, and
snuggle down before the fire with a good pipe (there's
tobacco in Middle-earth, though never cigarettes). But
the hobbits are curiously exempt from the cravings of
the flesh. Bilbo and Frodo are lifelong bachelors; indeed, there's only one female hobbit in the books, and
she comes on in the final pages as a bone to be tossed
to Sam the faithful retainer. Apart from this necessary
exemption, hobbitry is a boy's club.

Moreover, dynastic marriages among the big folk are
chilly to the point of appearing odd. Aragorn marries
a faceless creature for the occasion (having become a
king, he needs a queen), and Éowyn marries Faramir because she cannot get Aragorn. There are a couple of
ghostly, exquisite elf-ladies who live with Tom Bombadil
and Celeborn, but whether as sisters, wives, daughters,
or nature-sprites cannot be told. It is a rare moment
of feeling when the shy, gigantic, immensely old ents of
the deep forest express grief for their long-lost entwives. Indeed, Tolkien's avoidance of sex is striking;
given the mode of romance, it's a perfectly legitimate
avoidance, but can't fail to heighten the sense of in-
fantilism in the fantasy.

A major element contributing to the appeal of the
Tolkien series may be the notion of Middle-earth as a
complete and self-sufficient place. Like the worlds of
the *Faerie Queene* or even *Star Wars,* like Oz and the
prophetic books of Blake, Middle-earth has flora, fauna,
and natural laws of its own, and it stands in an ever-
shifting, never-failing relation to our own earth. The
exotic visual effects and rich linguistic textures absorb the reader's attention and prevent him from feeling
the simplistic poverty of Tolkien's moralism, the repet-
itive monotony of the warfare. Tolkien's strong points
are names and creatures; he's endlessly fertile in the
creation of both. On the whole, he doesn't invent new

laws of nature, but animates old ones, particularly
those of sympathetic magic, if laws they can be called.
   With battles, sieges, and travels he's less at ease,
and shows it by repeating certain stock effects. The
siege of Isengard is very like the siege of Gondor;
again and again the heroes are called on to crawl
through dark and perilous — and practically identical —
underground passages to which Agnew's wisdom applies —
when you've seen one tunnel, you've seen 'em all. And
the hobbits take an inordinate number of forced marches
cross-country, which exhaust not only the little creatures but the reader. Still, it is a world in which one
can be caught up, with surprises and suspense to atone
for the occasional *longueurs,* and a reassuring sense
over all that Good is always good to its supporters and
will certainly prevail.
   Indeed, the success of Tolkien's books may need no
more explanation than this, that they contain a number
of extremely good stories which many readers seem to
be encountering for the first time. The books are a
pastiche of stories and scenes in which the reader encounters motifs from Genesis and Revelation, bits of
Beowulf, snatches of Wagner, pieces of Malory and of
MacPherson's *Ossian,* fragments of the sagas, Gaelic
legends, Breton lays, elements of the *Poema del Cid,* the
*Chanson de Roland, Orlando Furioso, The Faerie Queene,
Paradise Lost,* and more, much, much more. This rich
gallimaufry of narrative is softened here and melodram-
atized there for the modern taste, and exempt by being
a fairy tale from merely rational criticism. People
who have enjoyed it would be well advised not to try
prolonging the pleasure by studying *The Silmarillion.*
Instead, if the thought isn't too solemn, they might try
some of the books that Tolkien himself used to construct
his Disneyized cycle.